Playful Adventures
Coloring Book

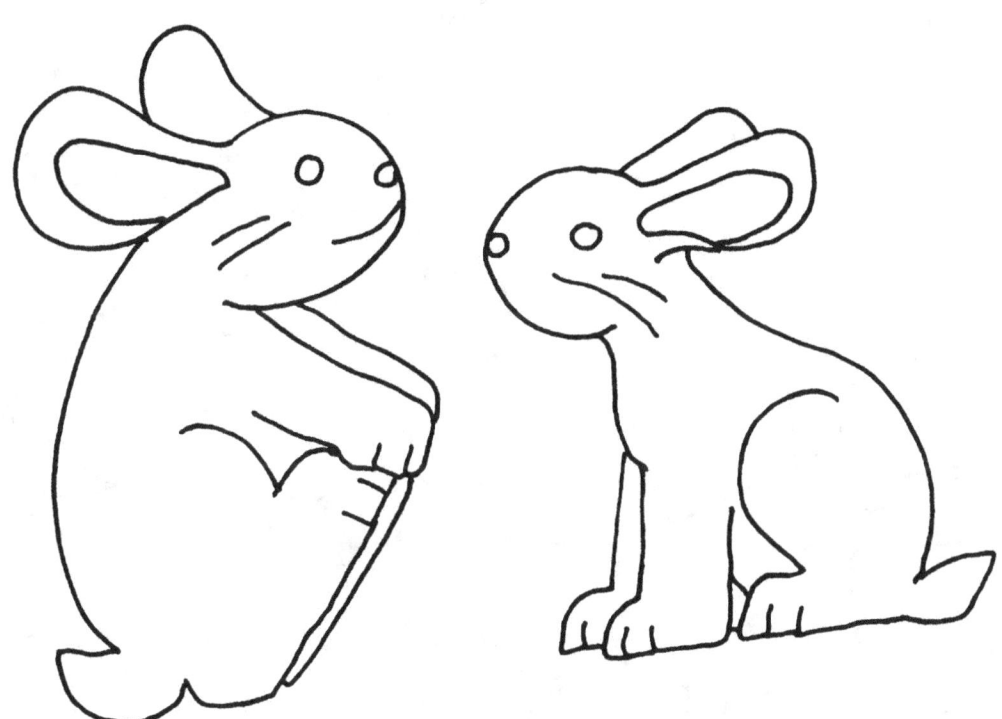

A Coloring Book for Everyone

DRAWINGS BY KIMBERLY GARVEY

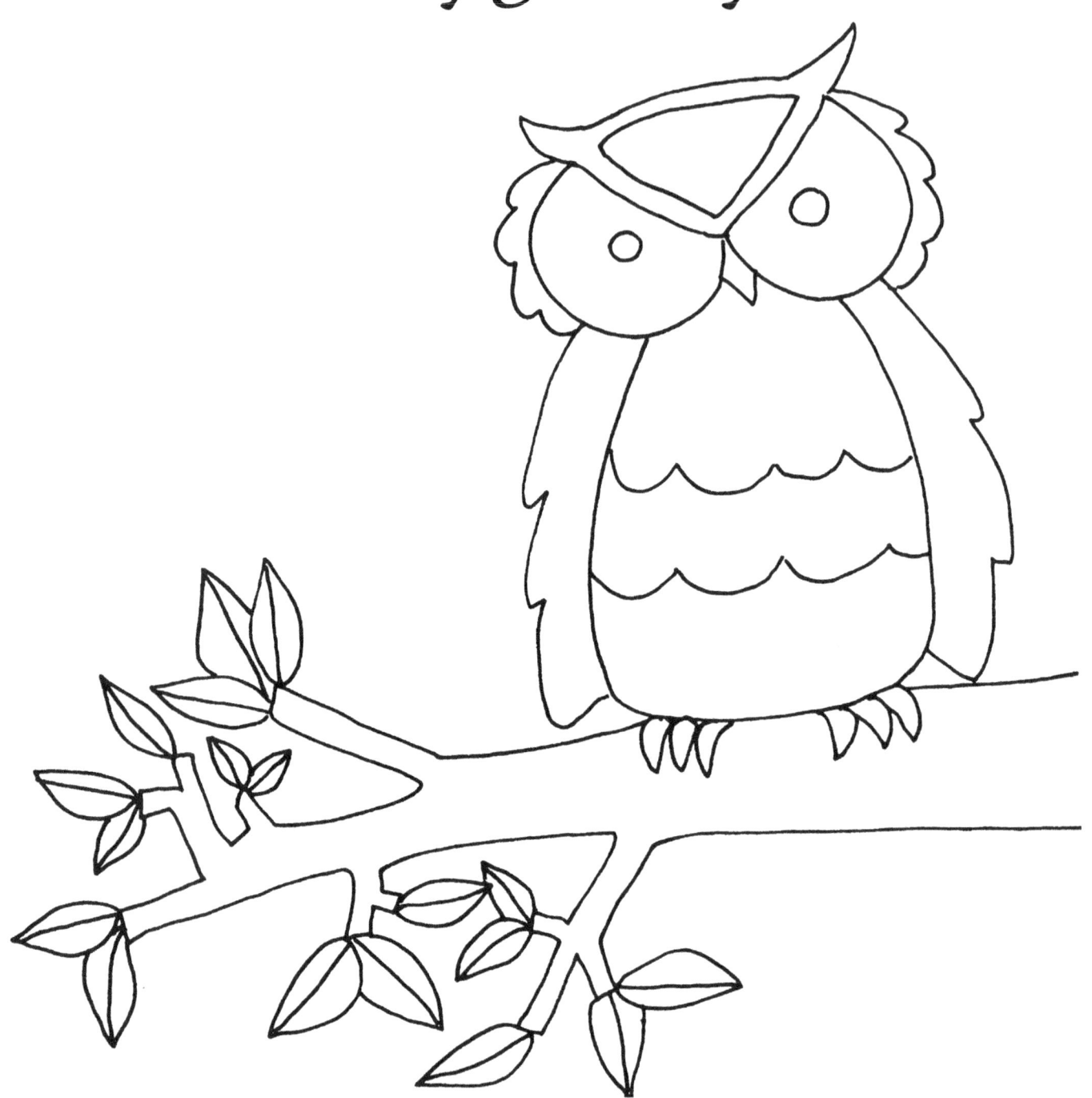

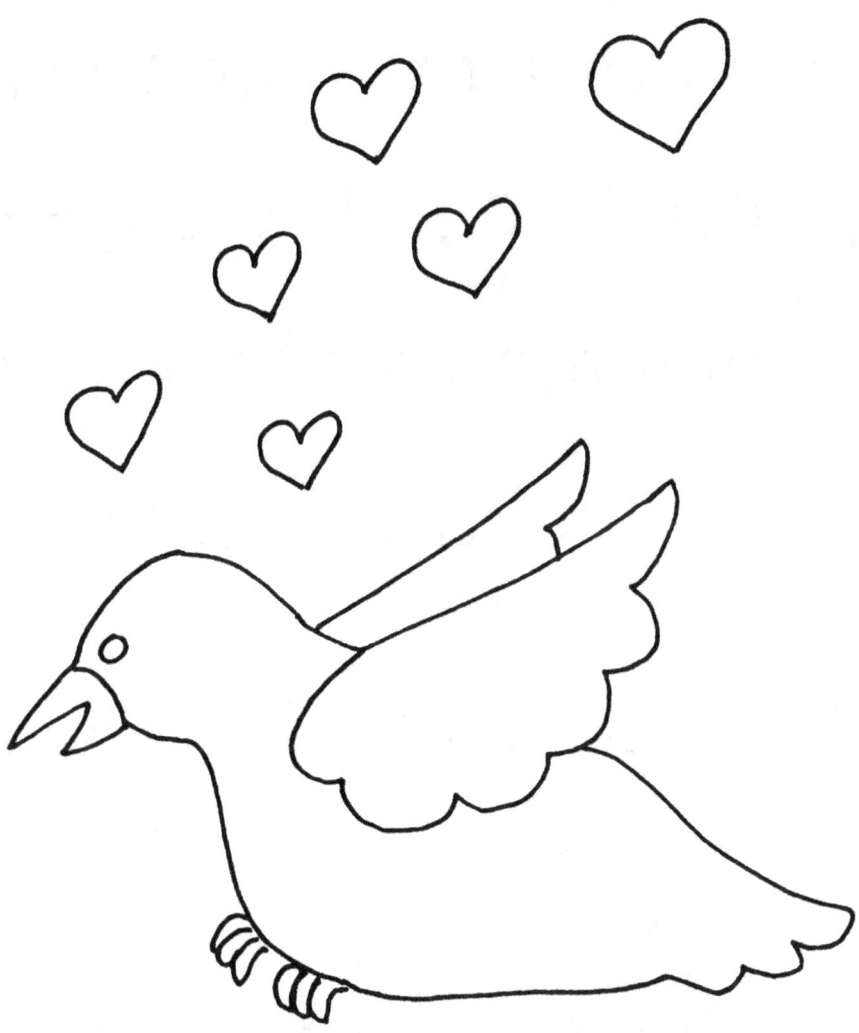

This book is dedicated to everyone who has supported me on my coloring book journey.

WARNING!!!!

Please put a protection sheet of paper between the pages when using markers to prevent bleed-through.

A protection sheet is included at the back of this book.

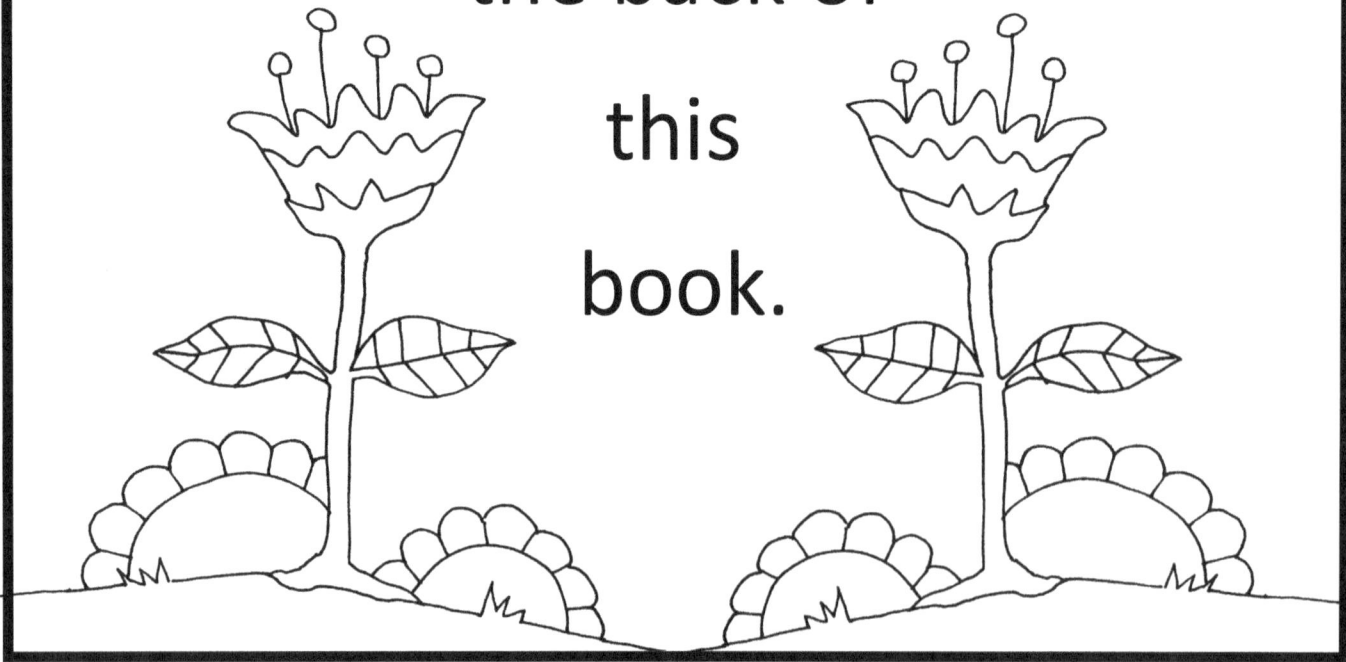

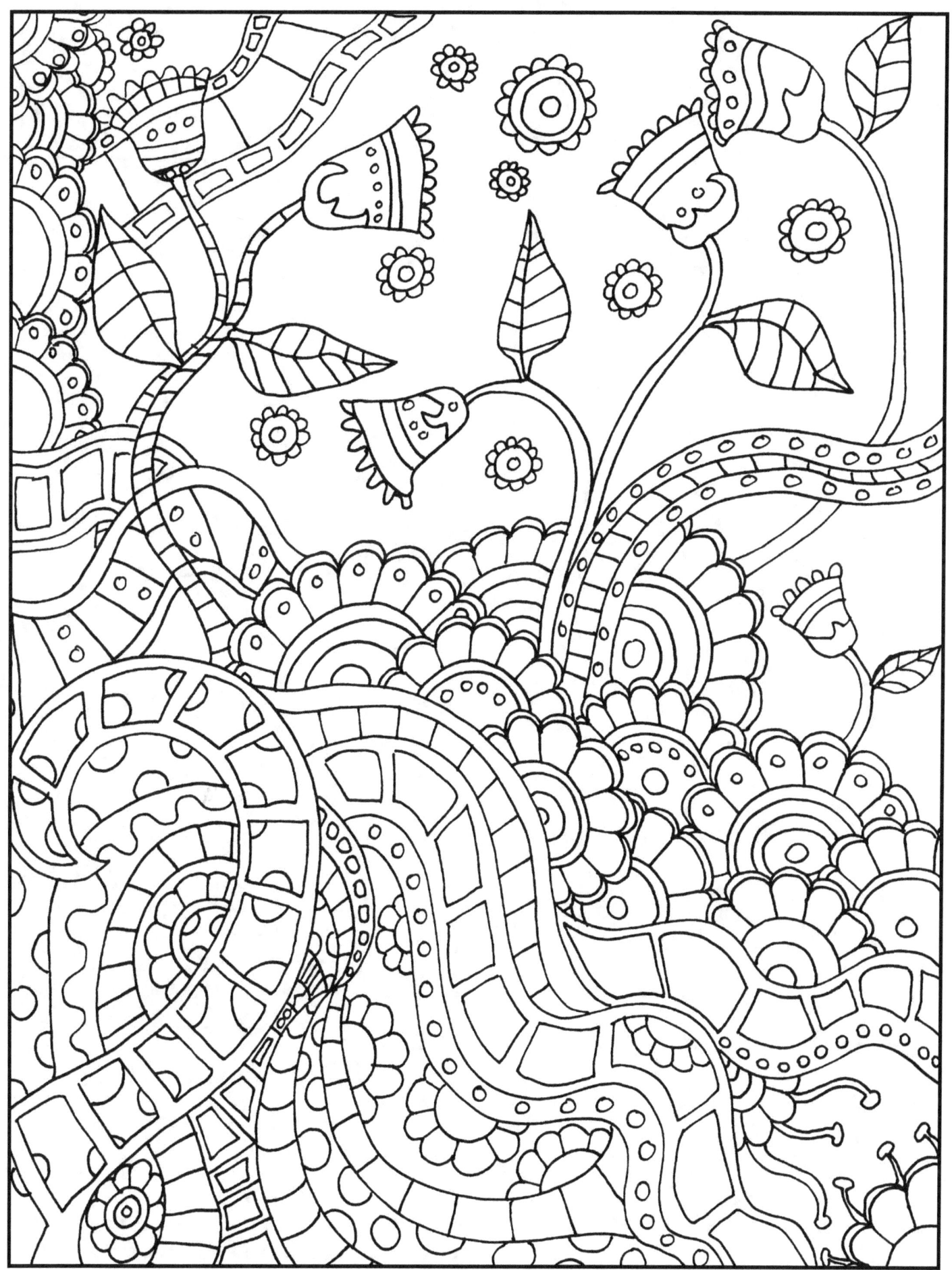

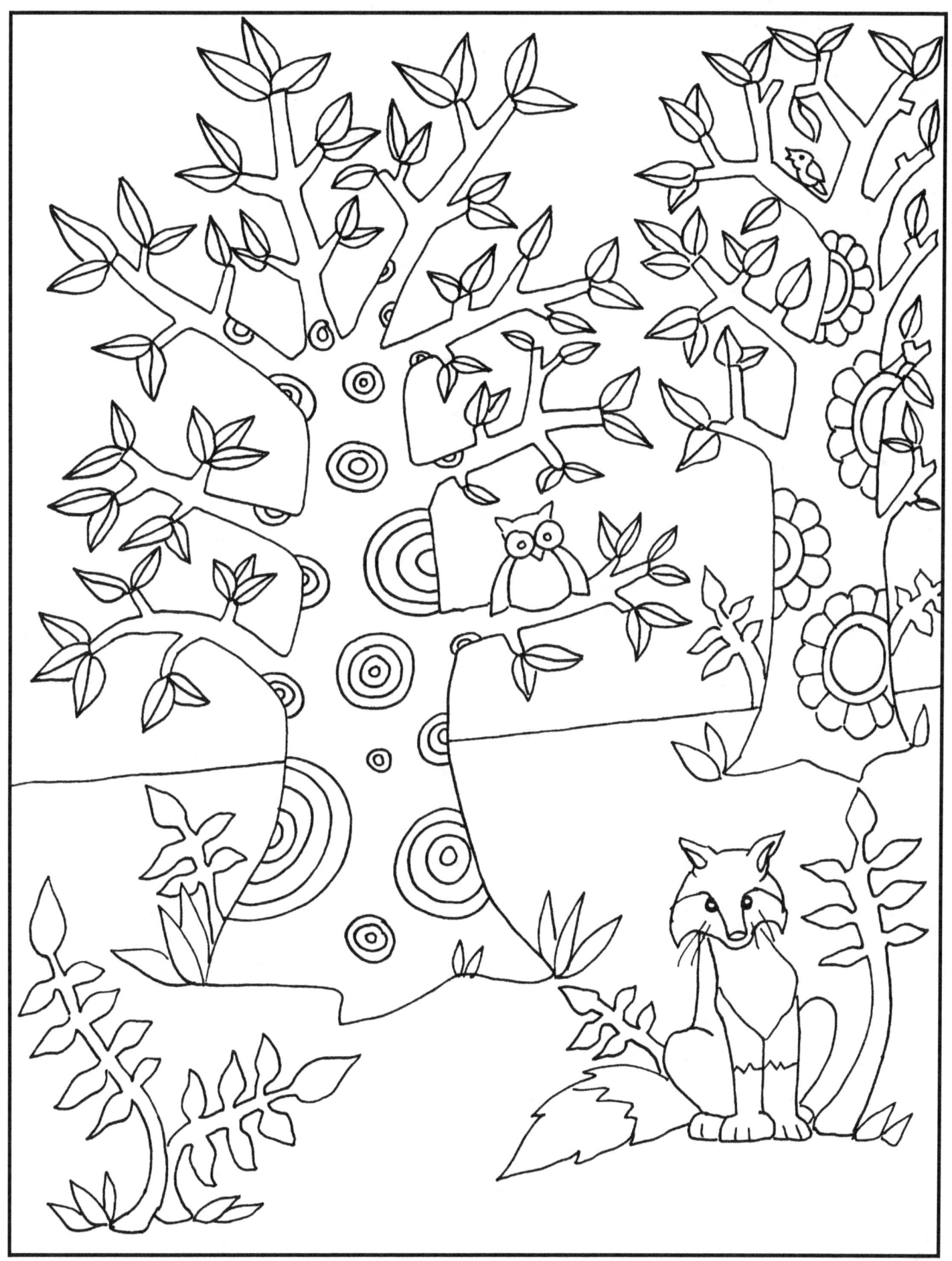

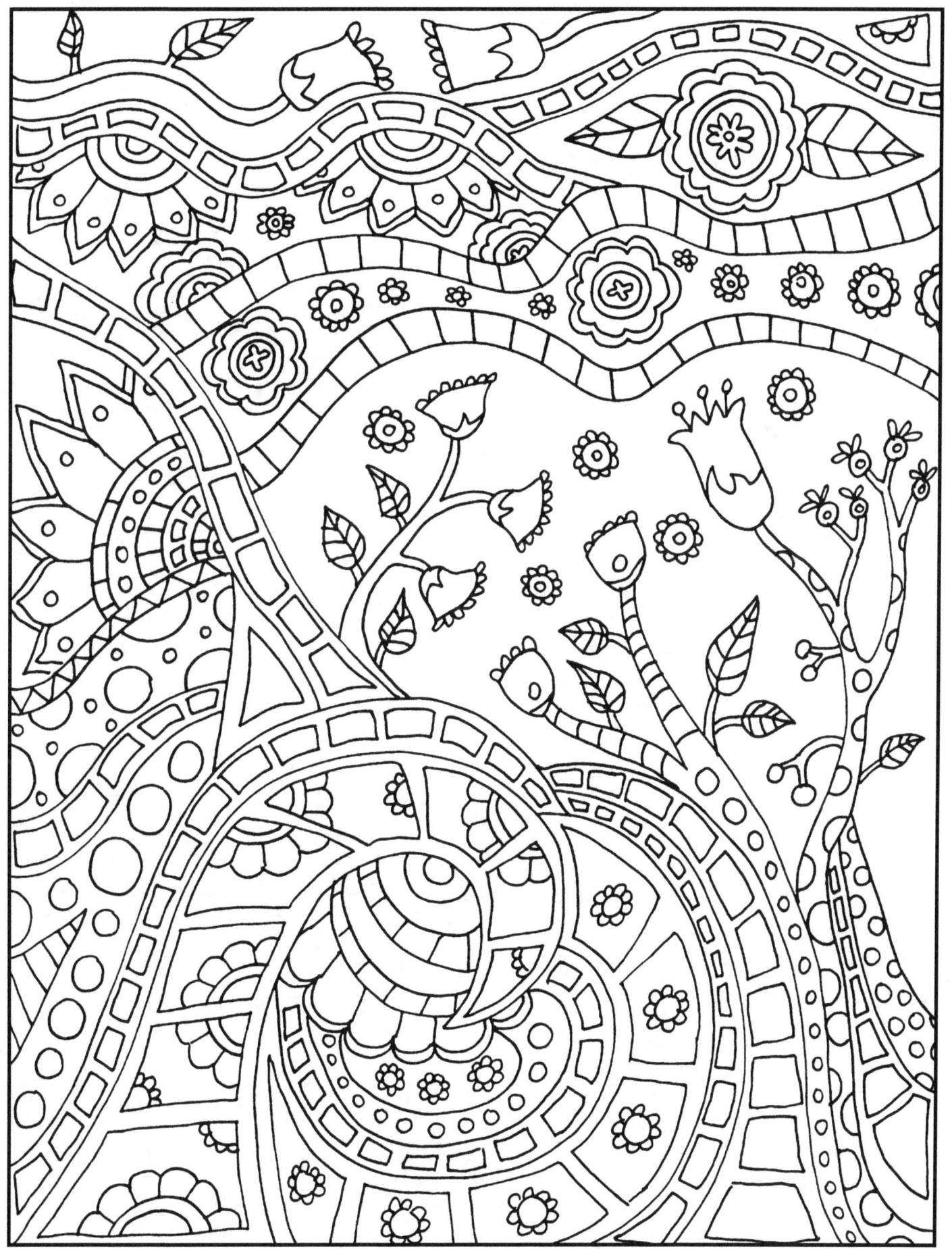

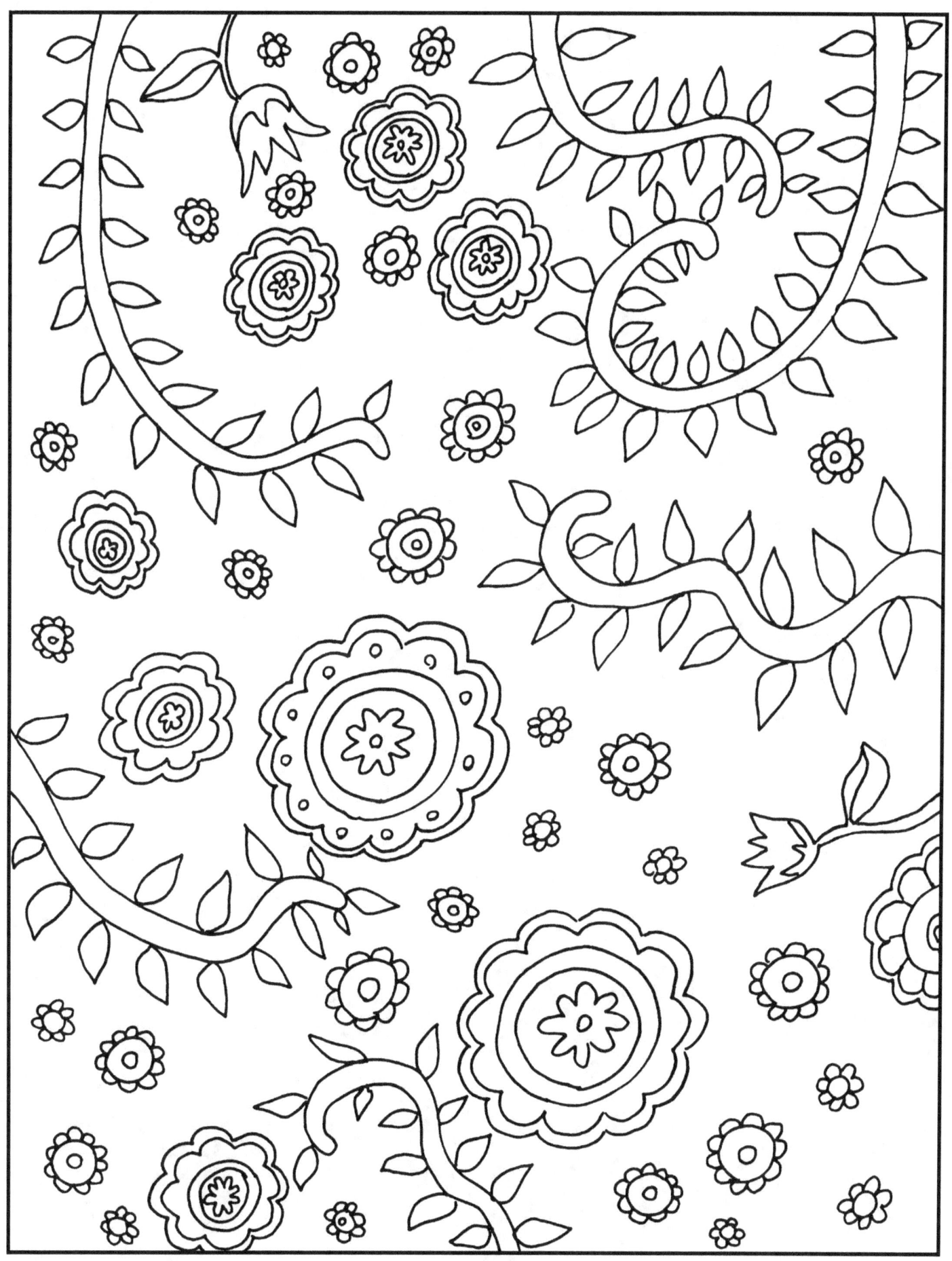

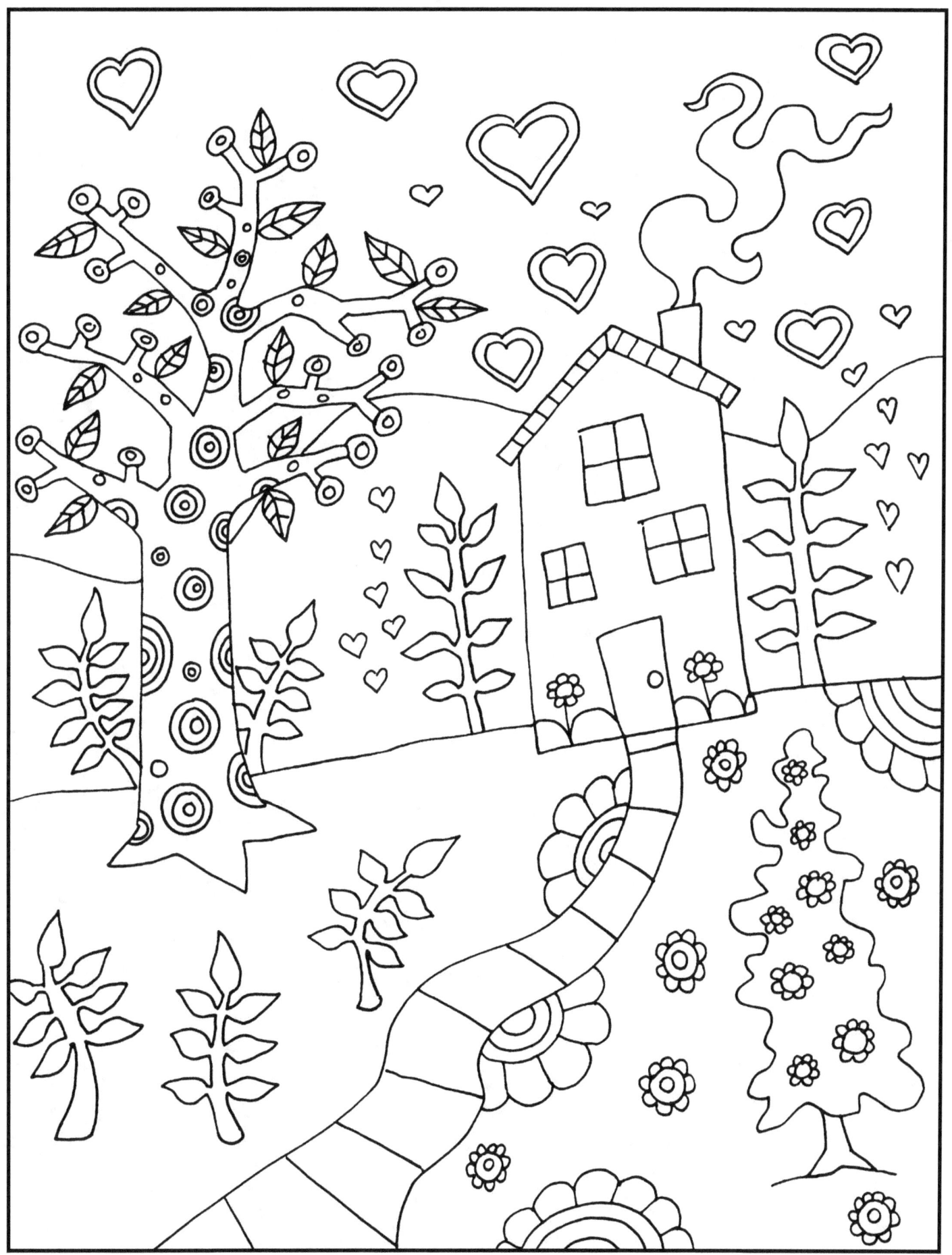

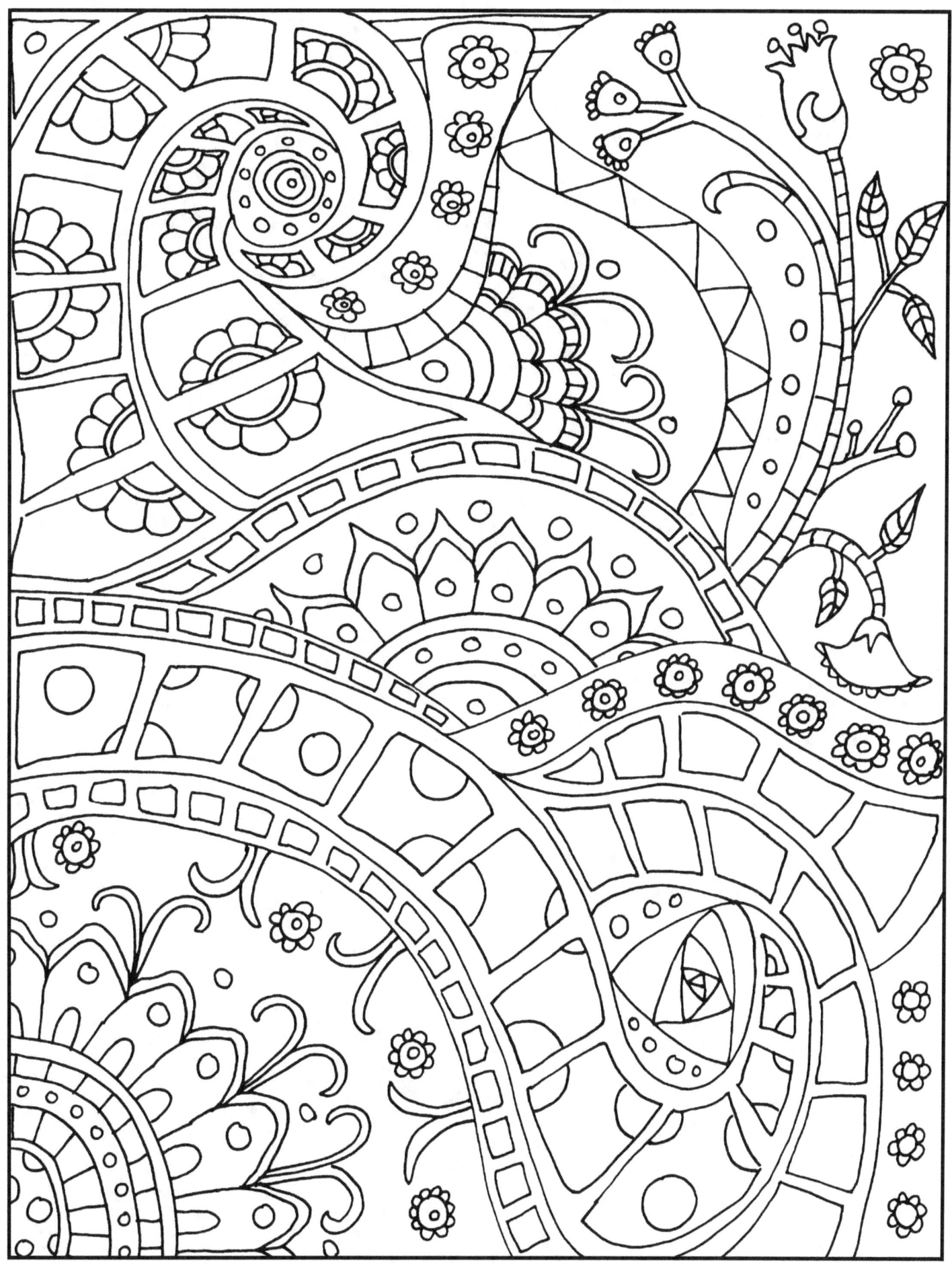

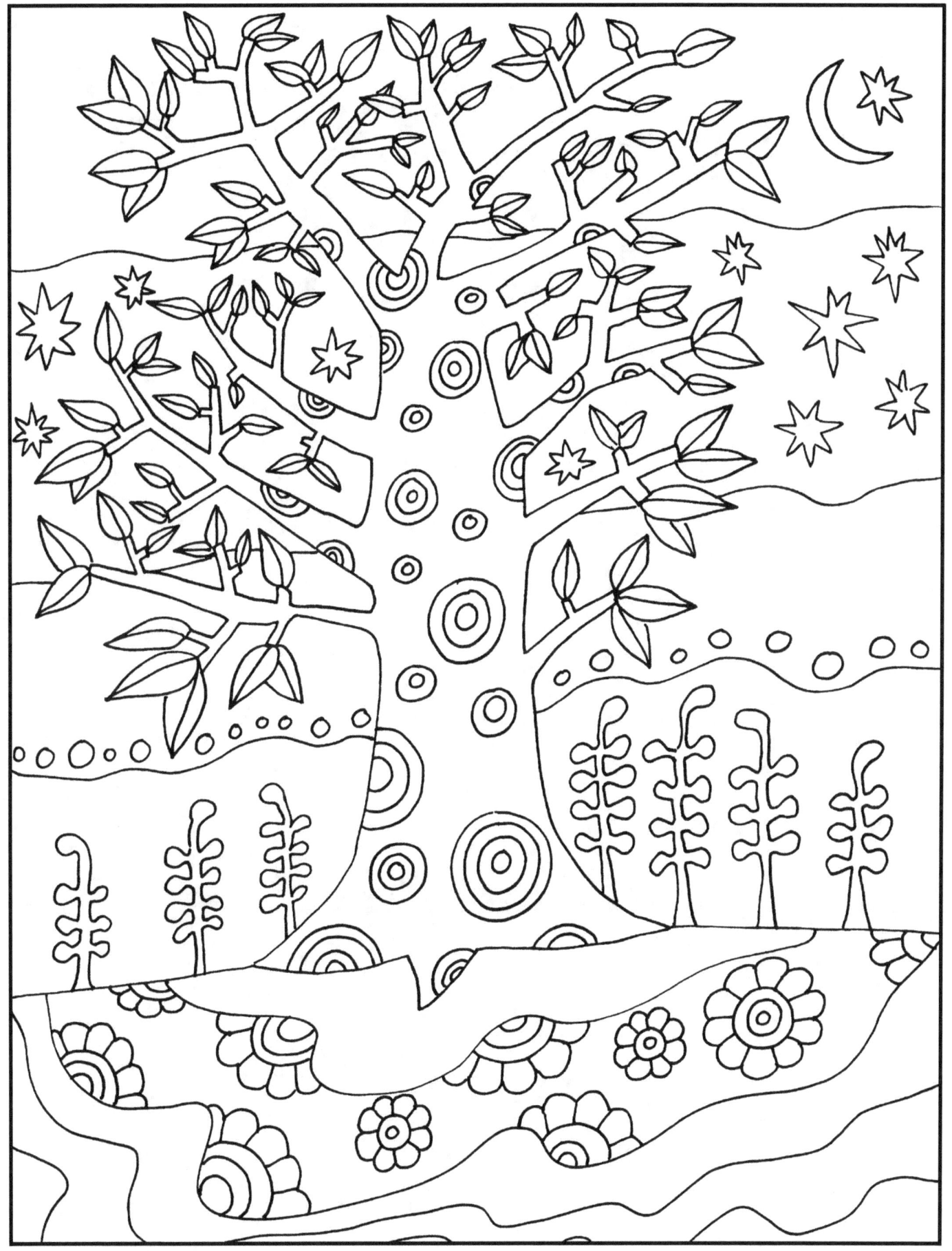

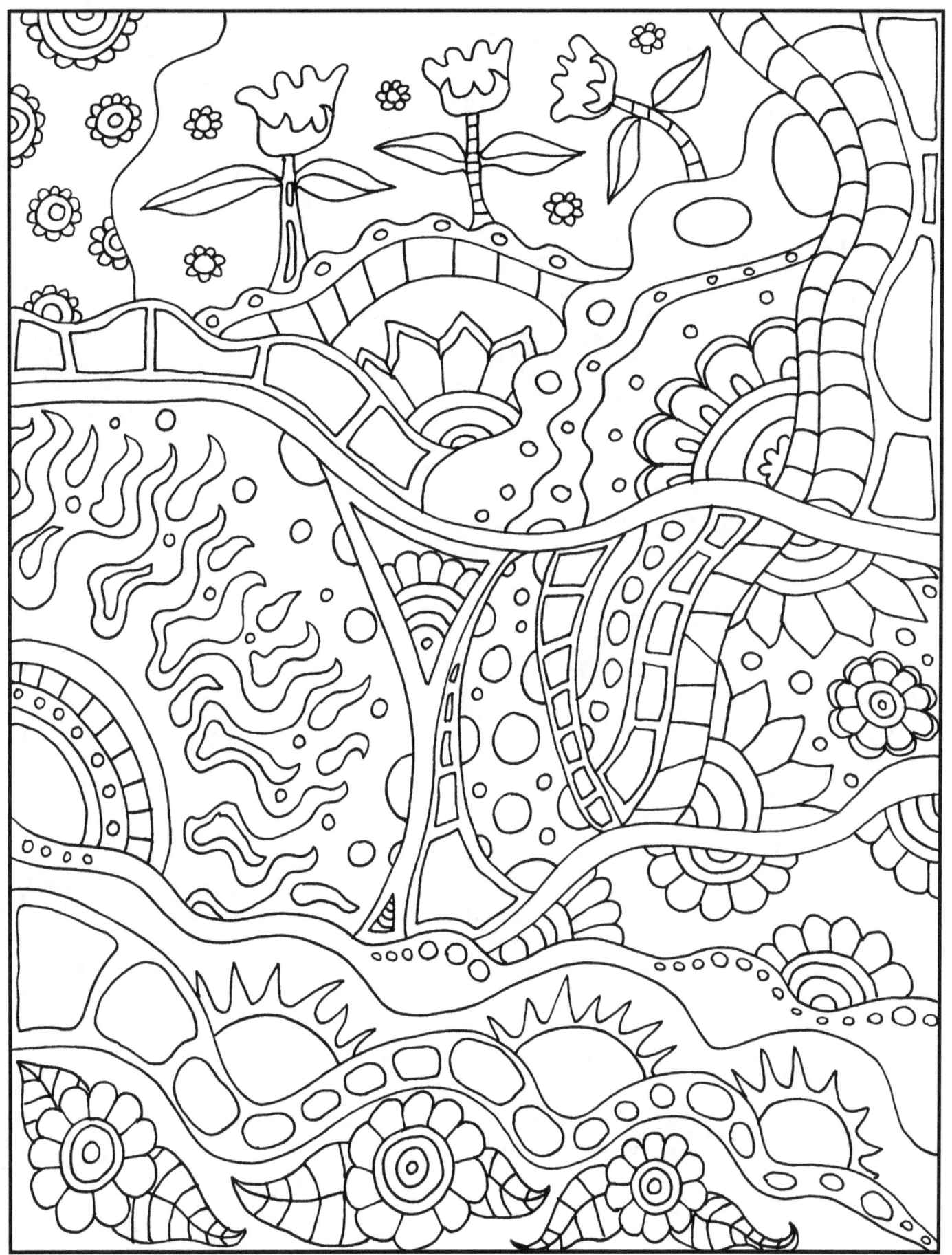

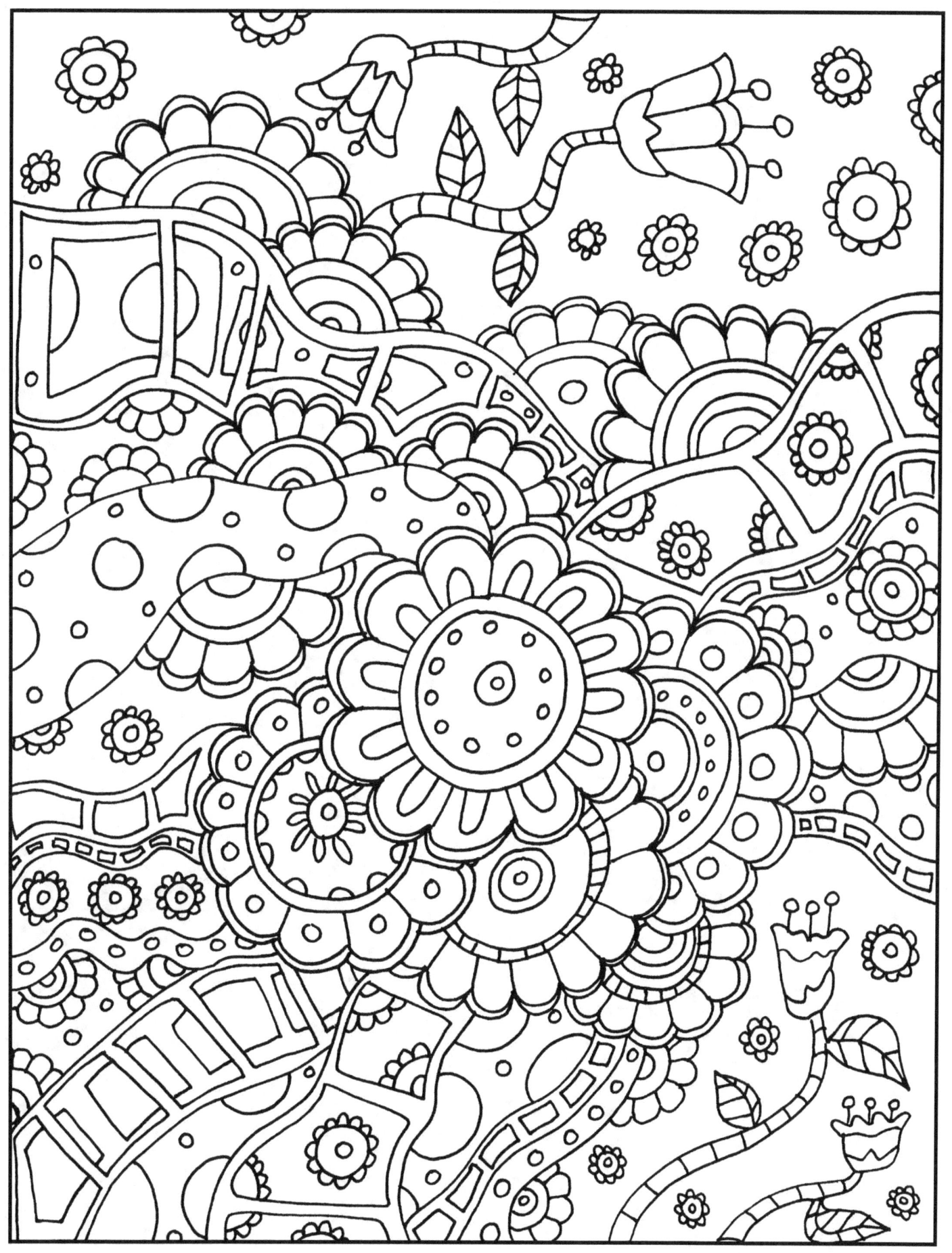

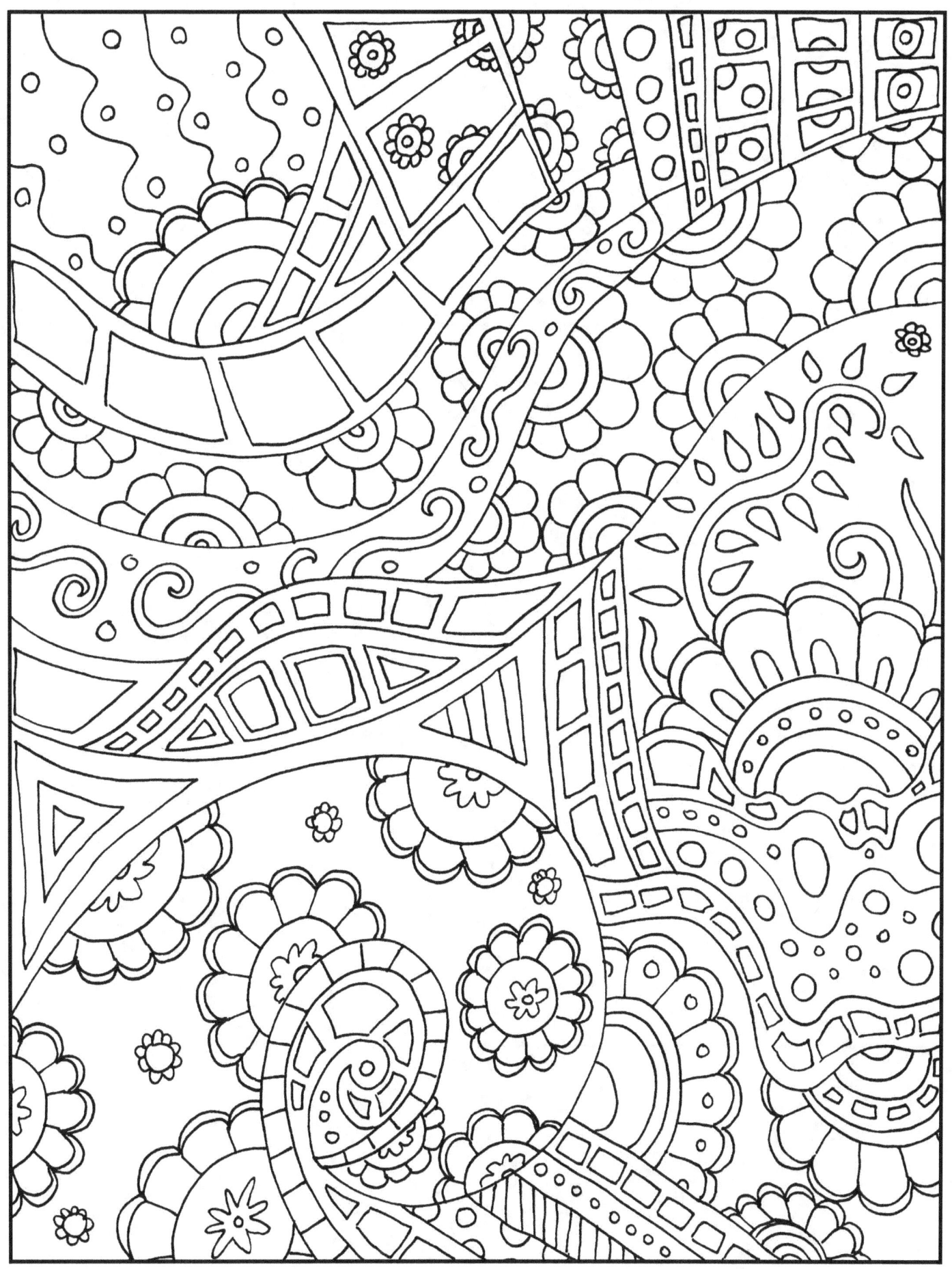

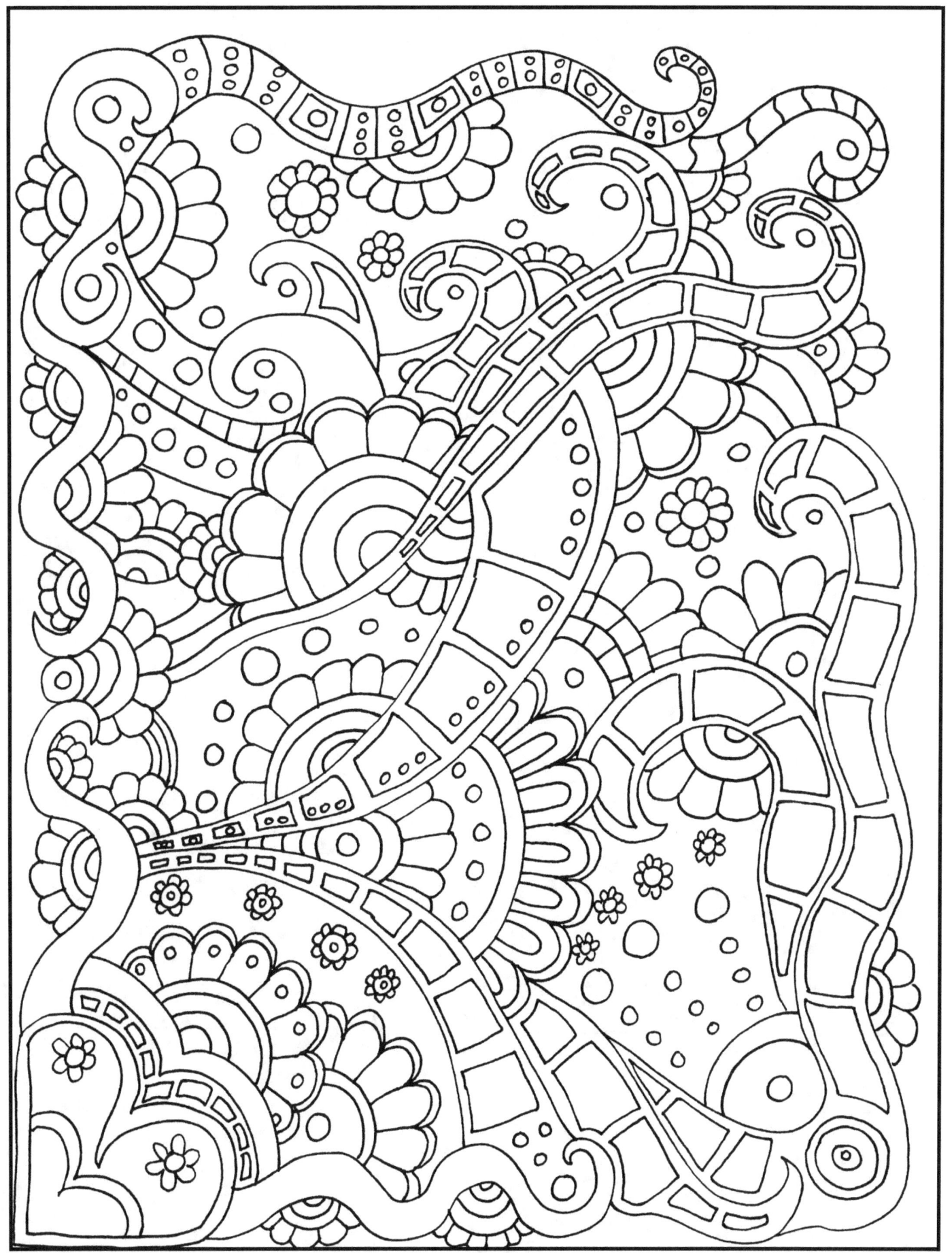

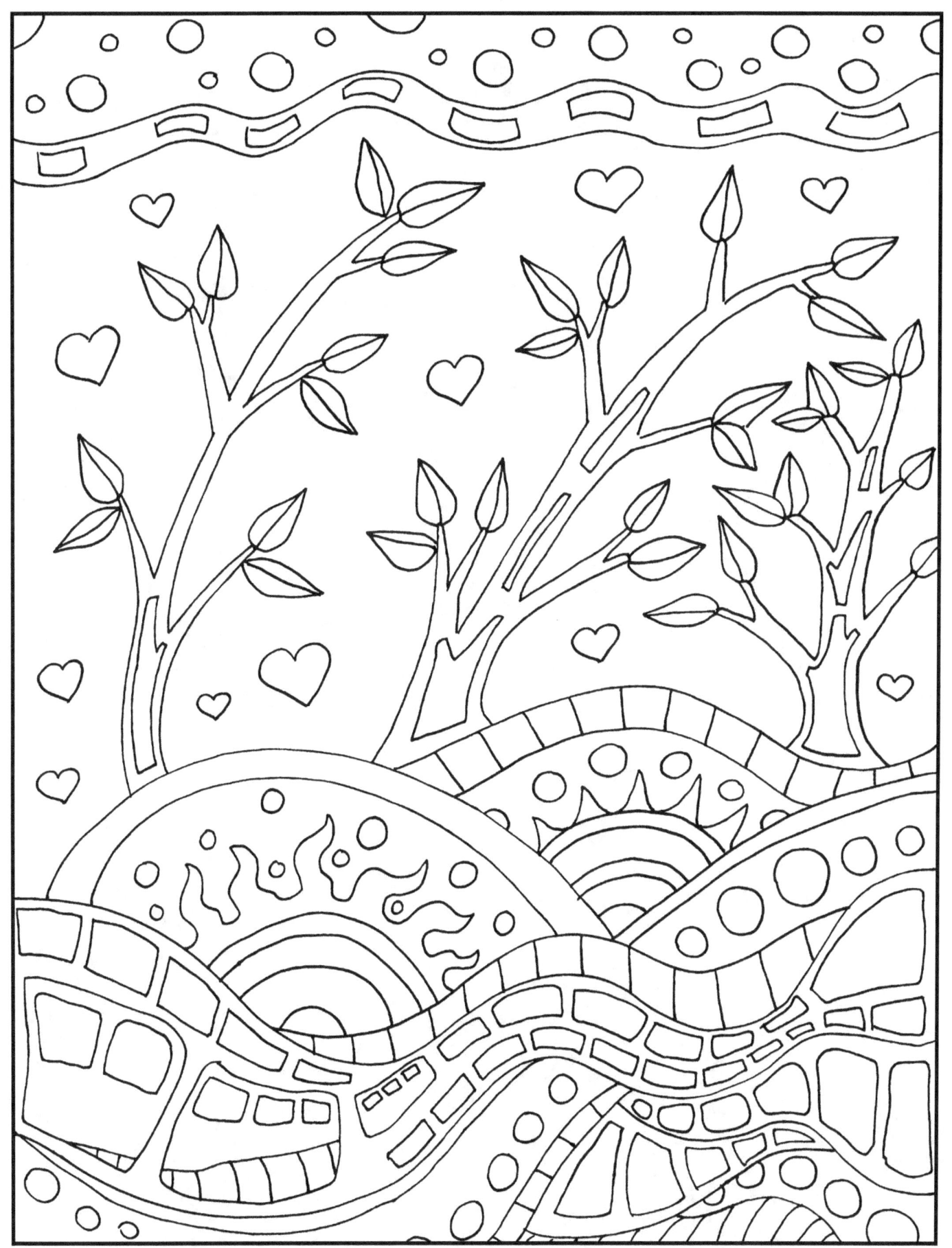

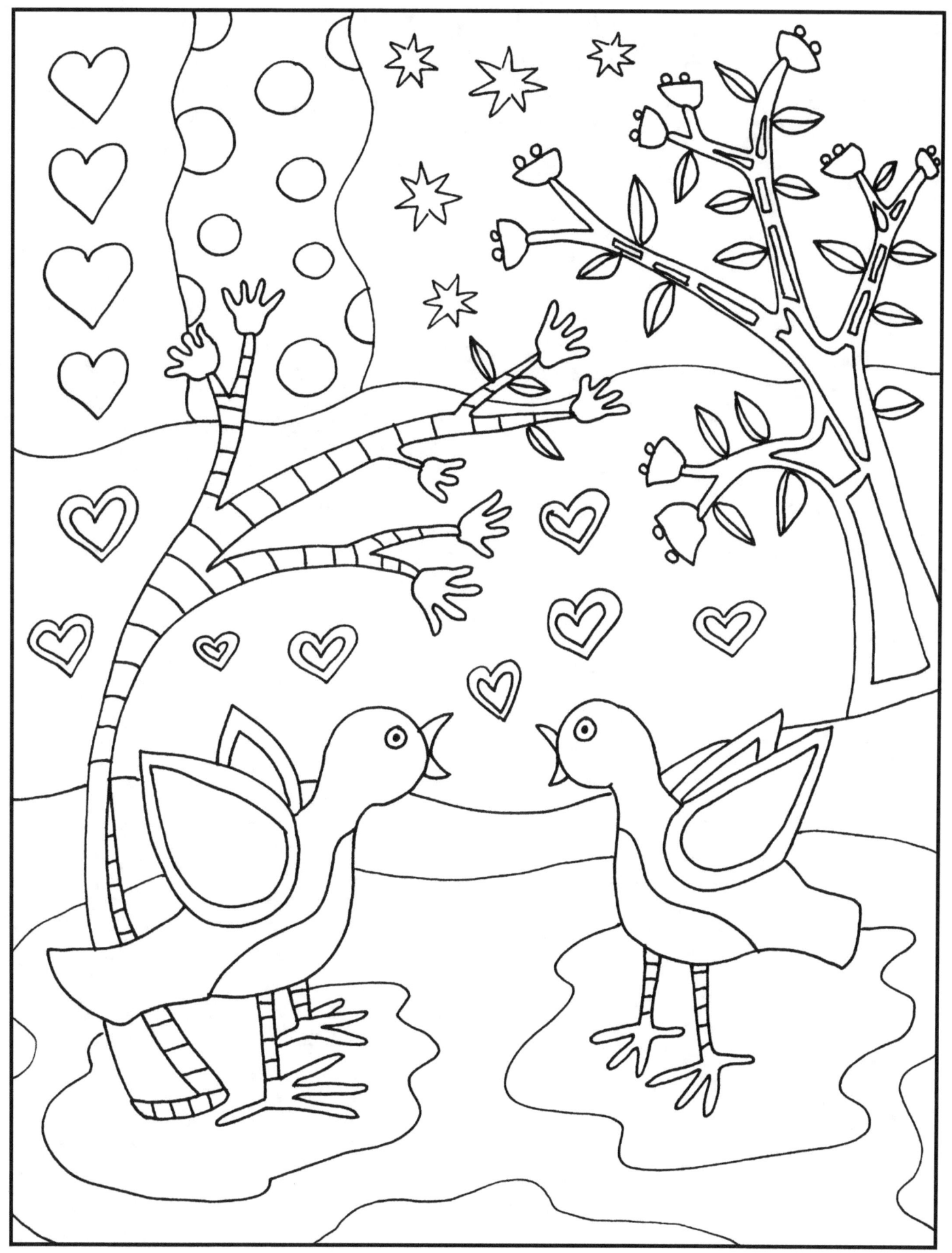

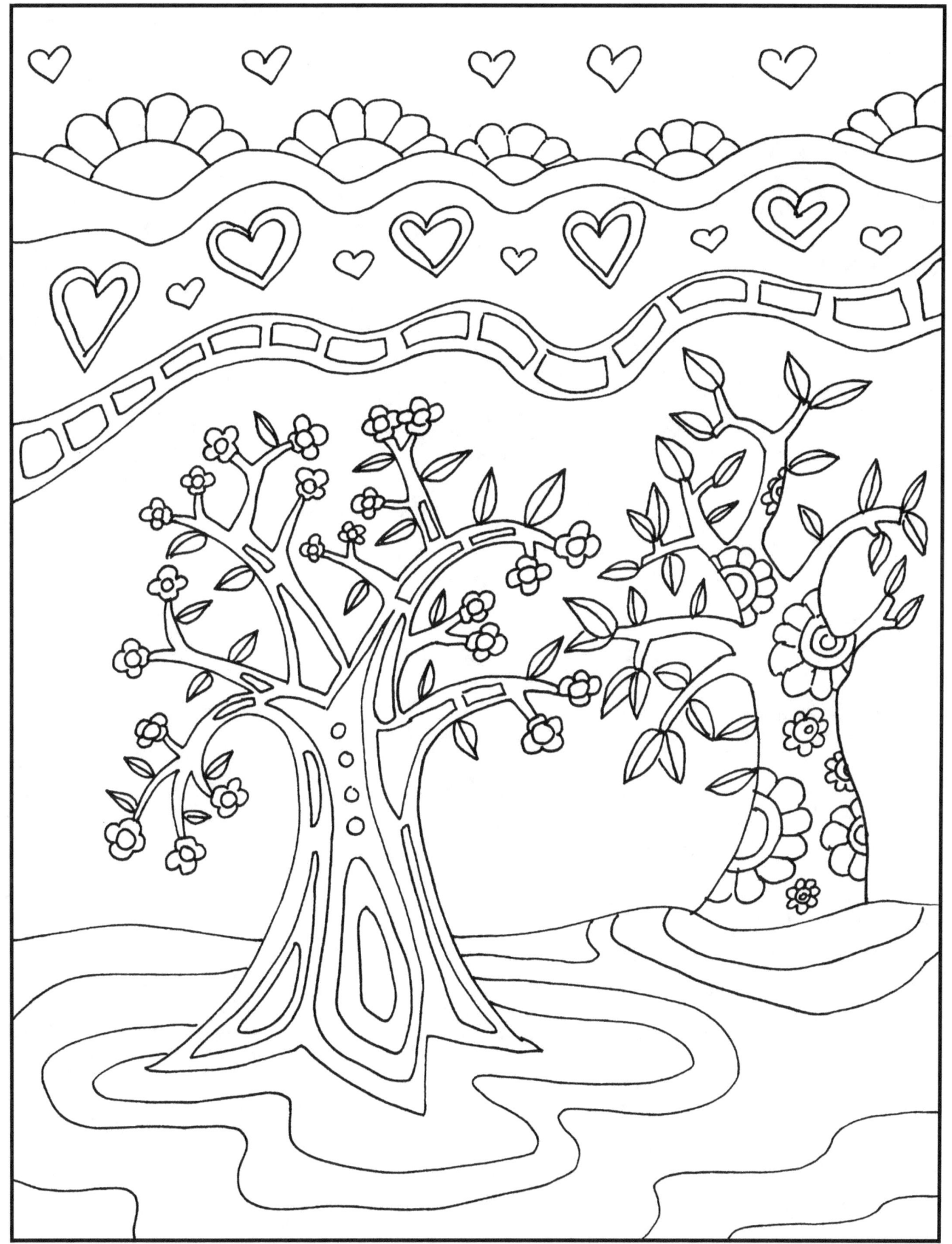

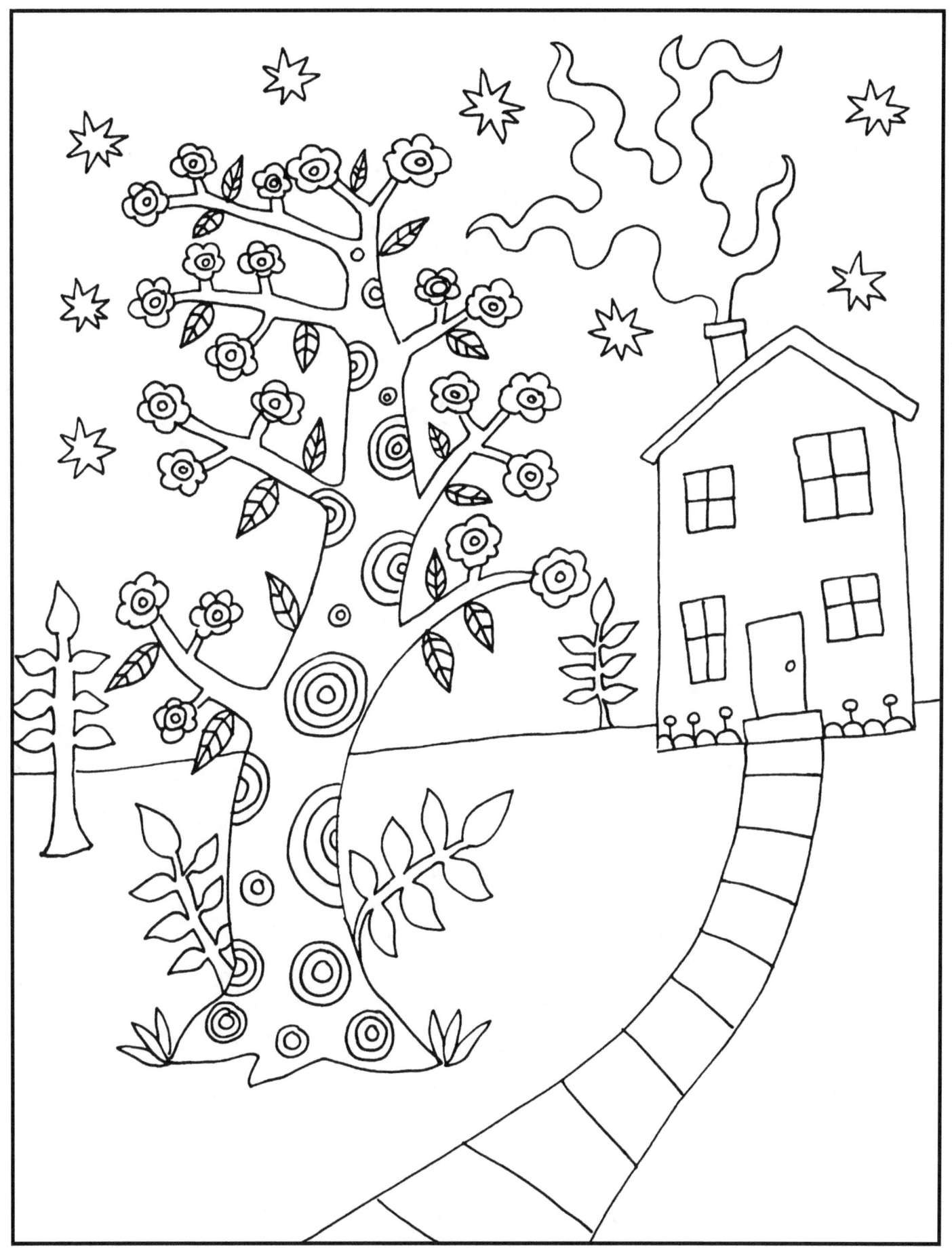

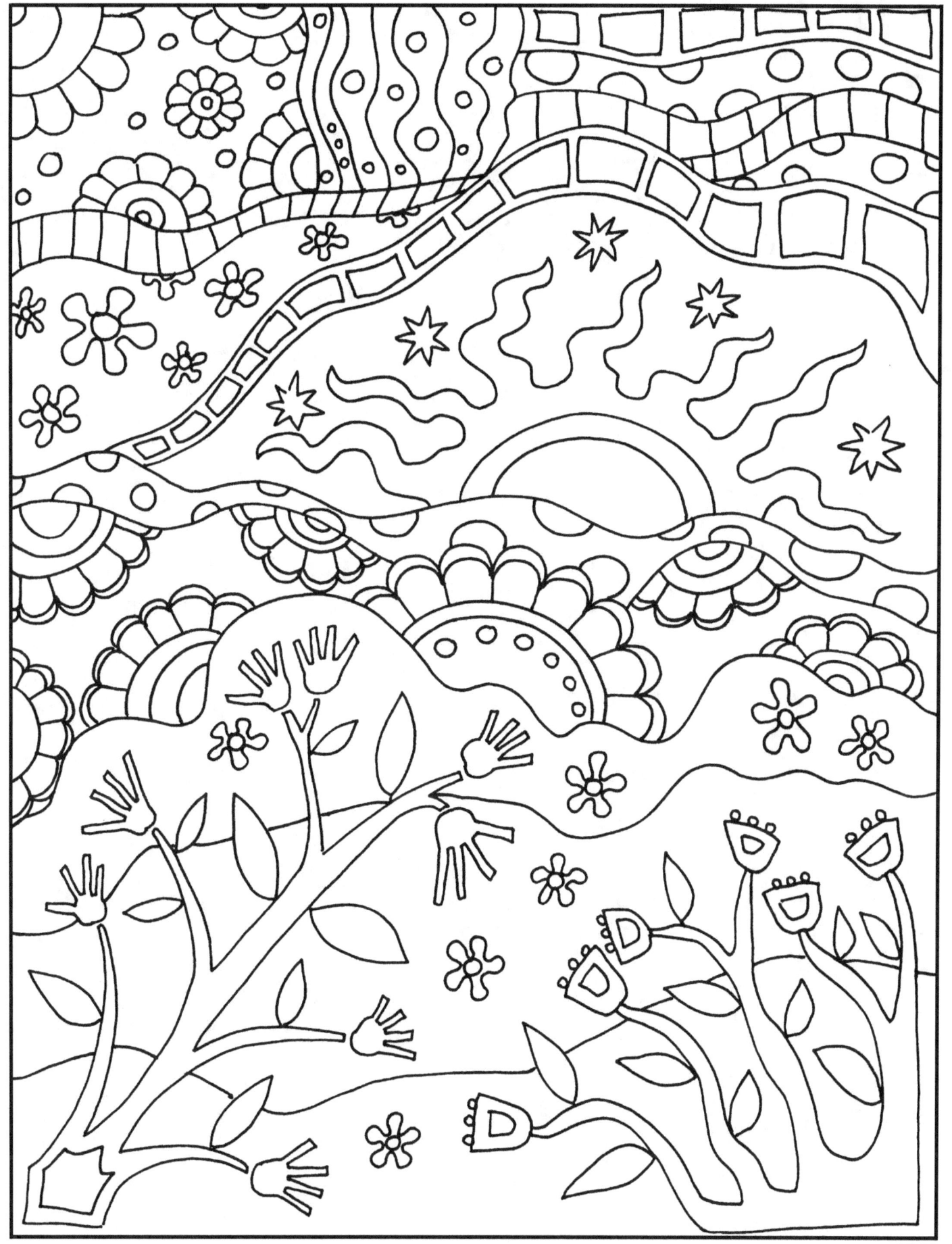

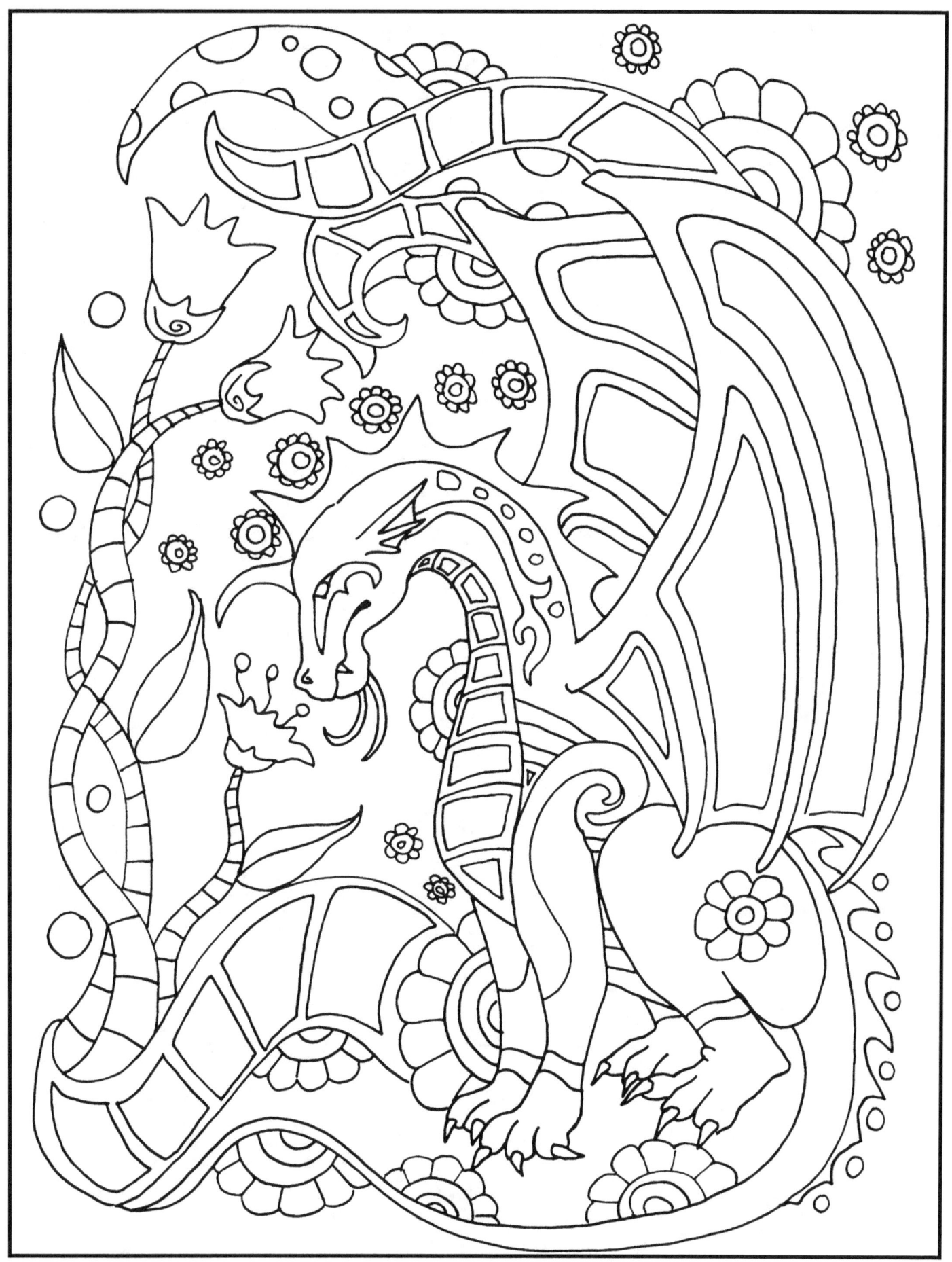

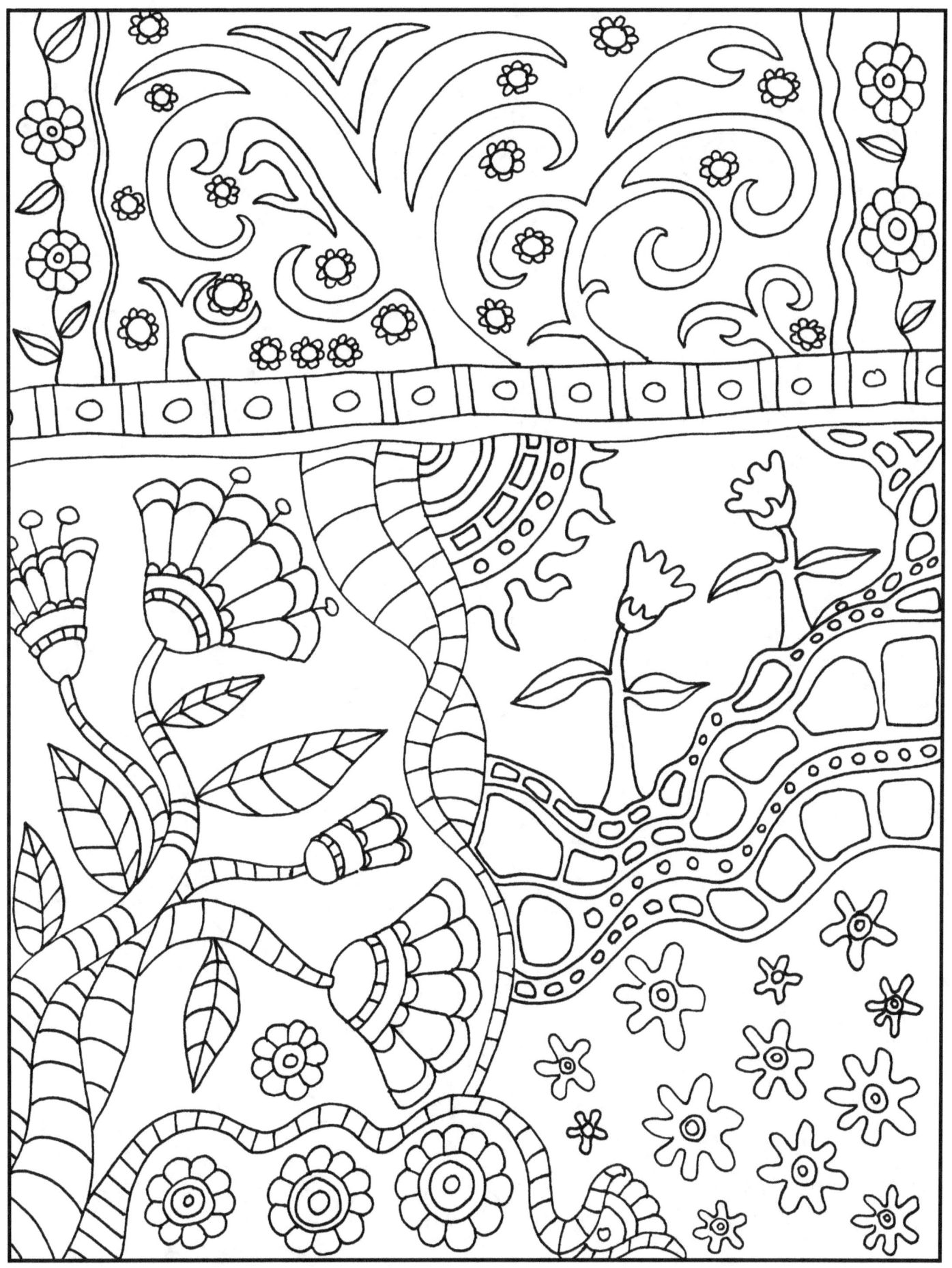

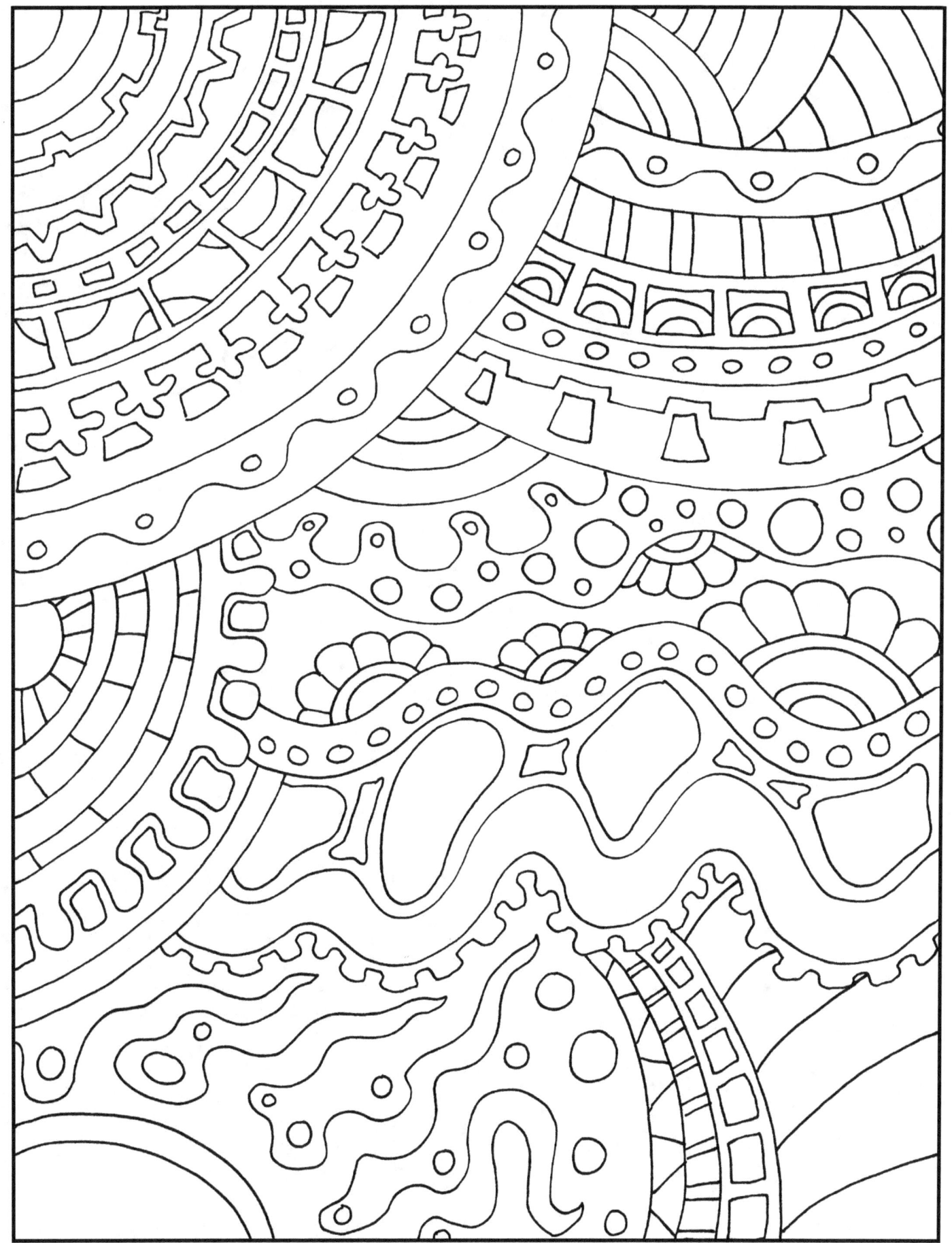

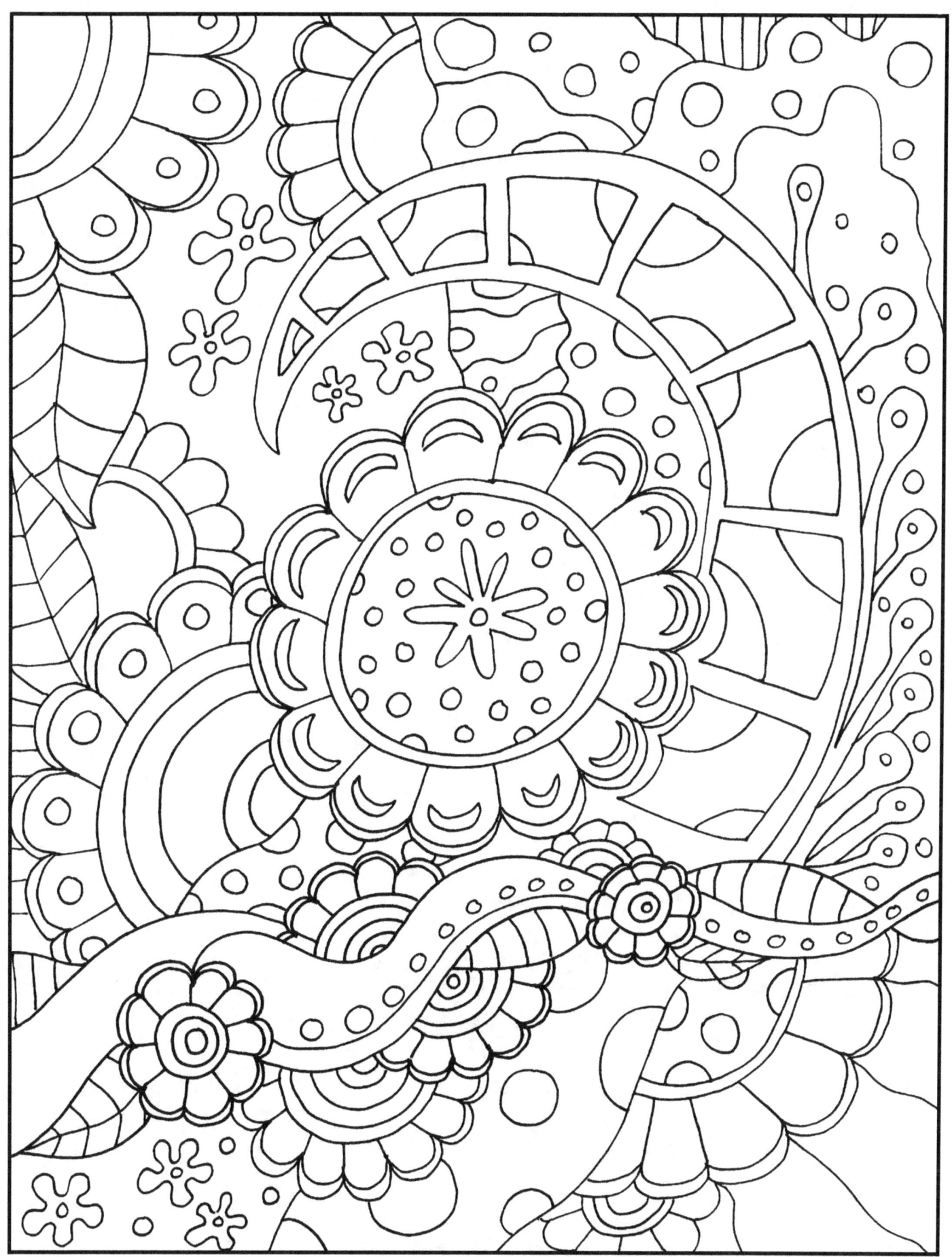

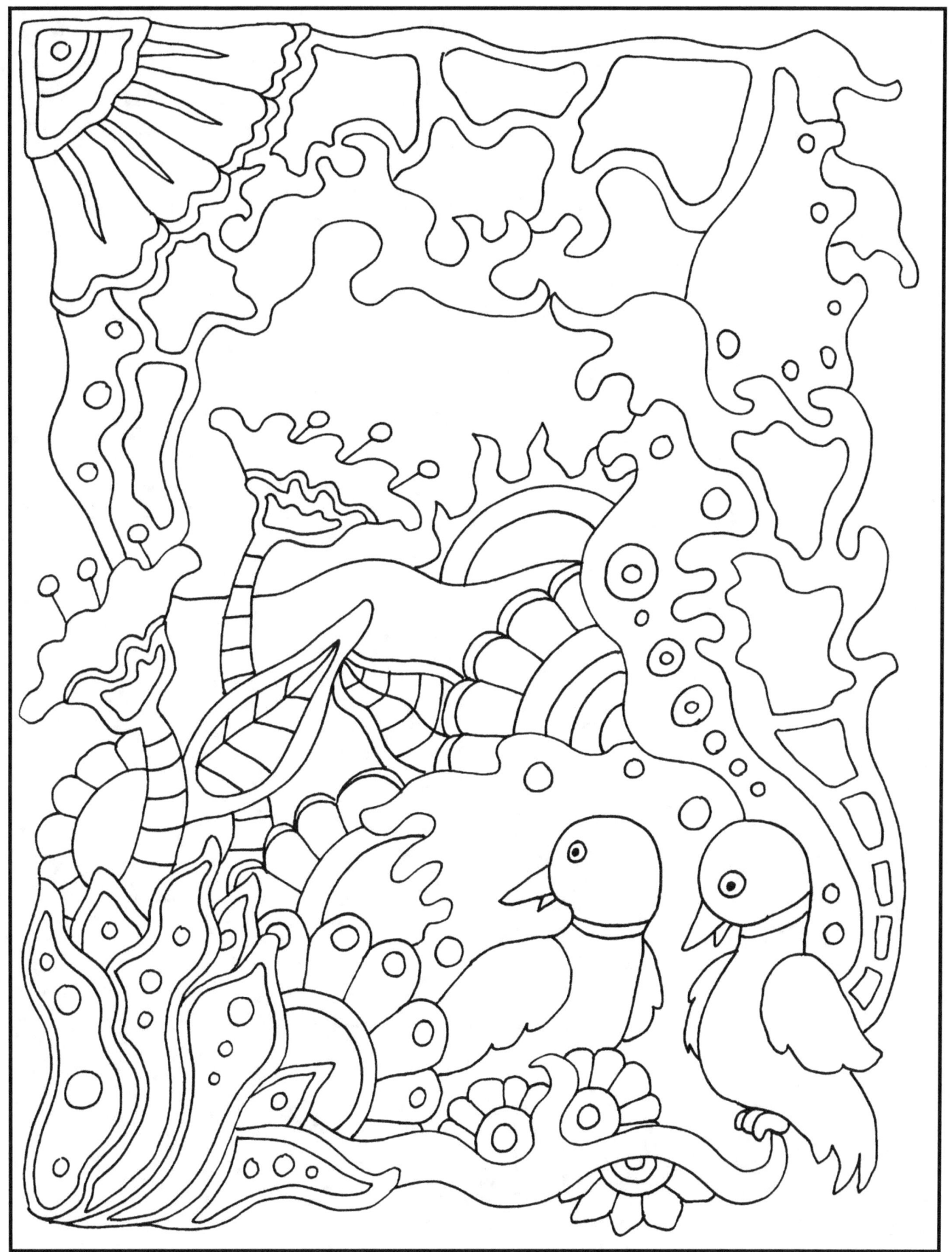

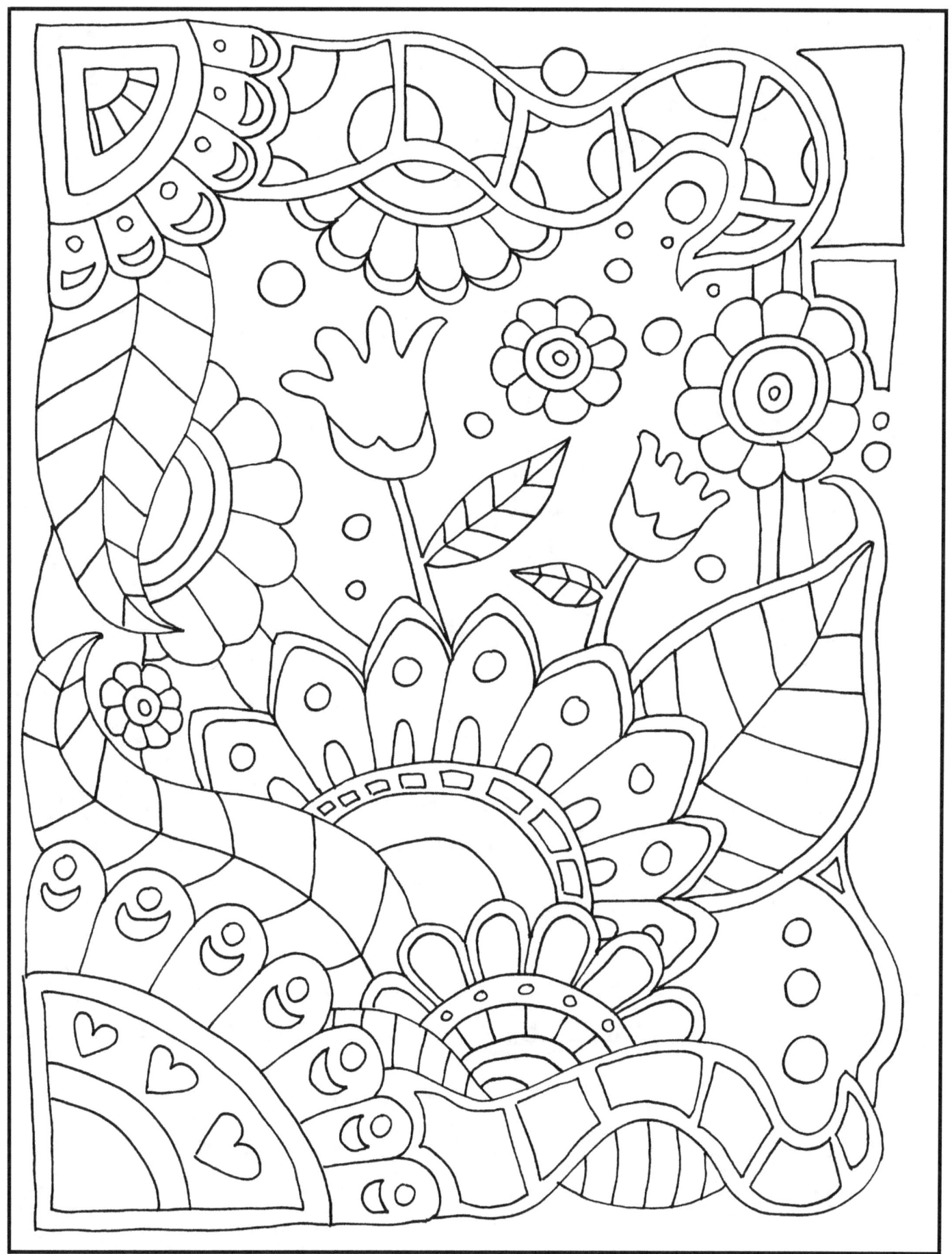

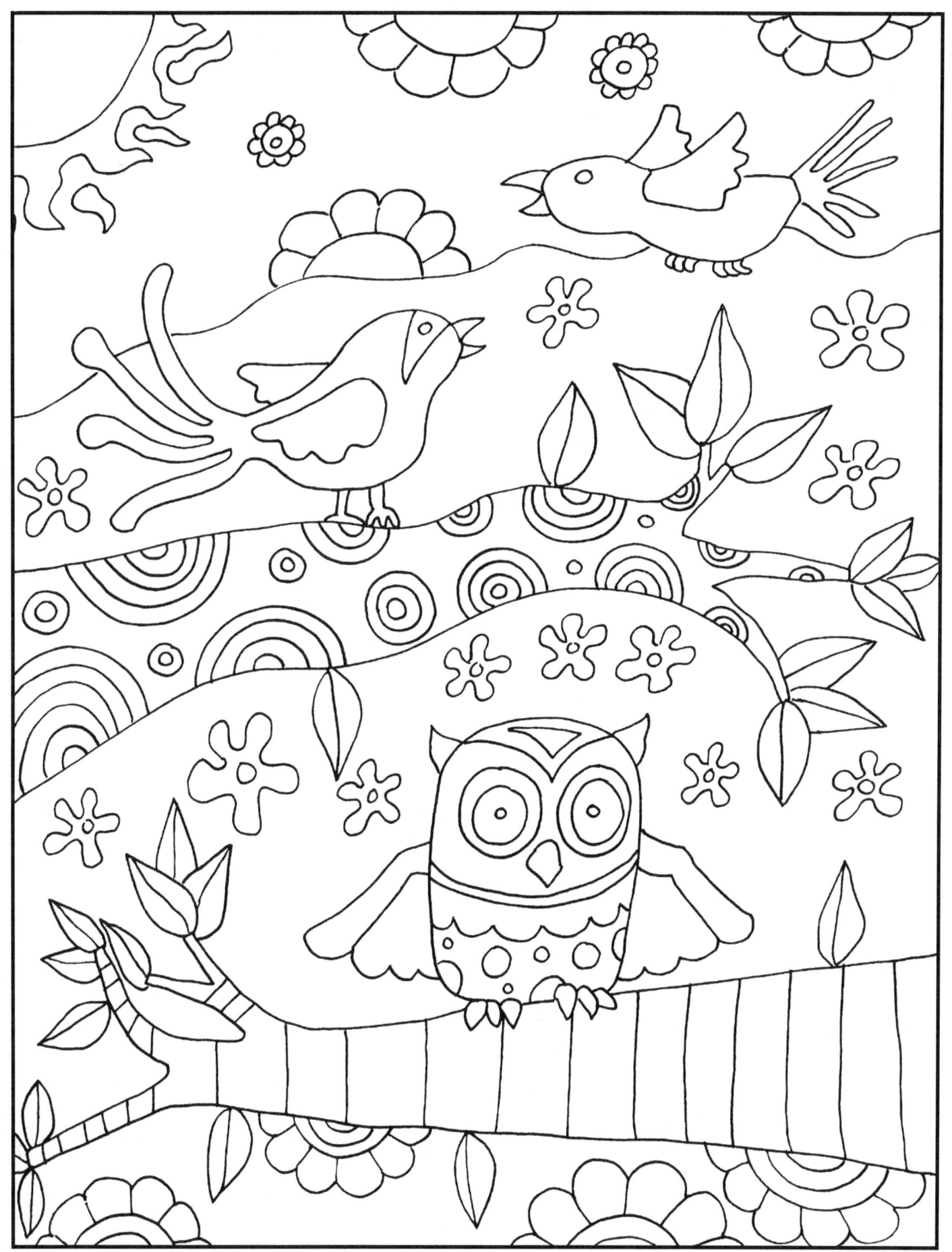

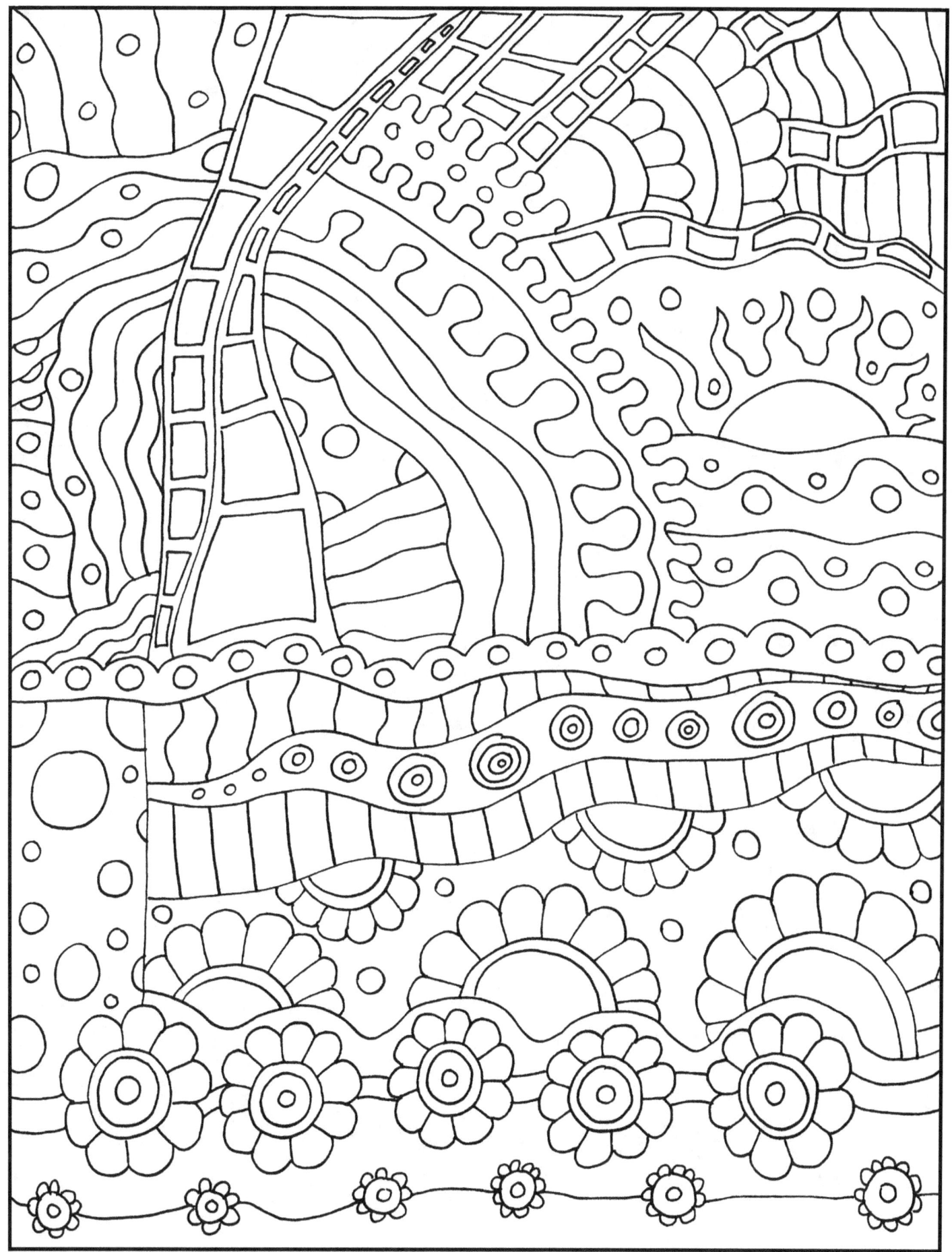

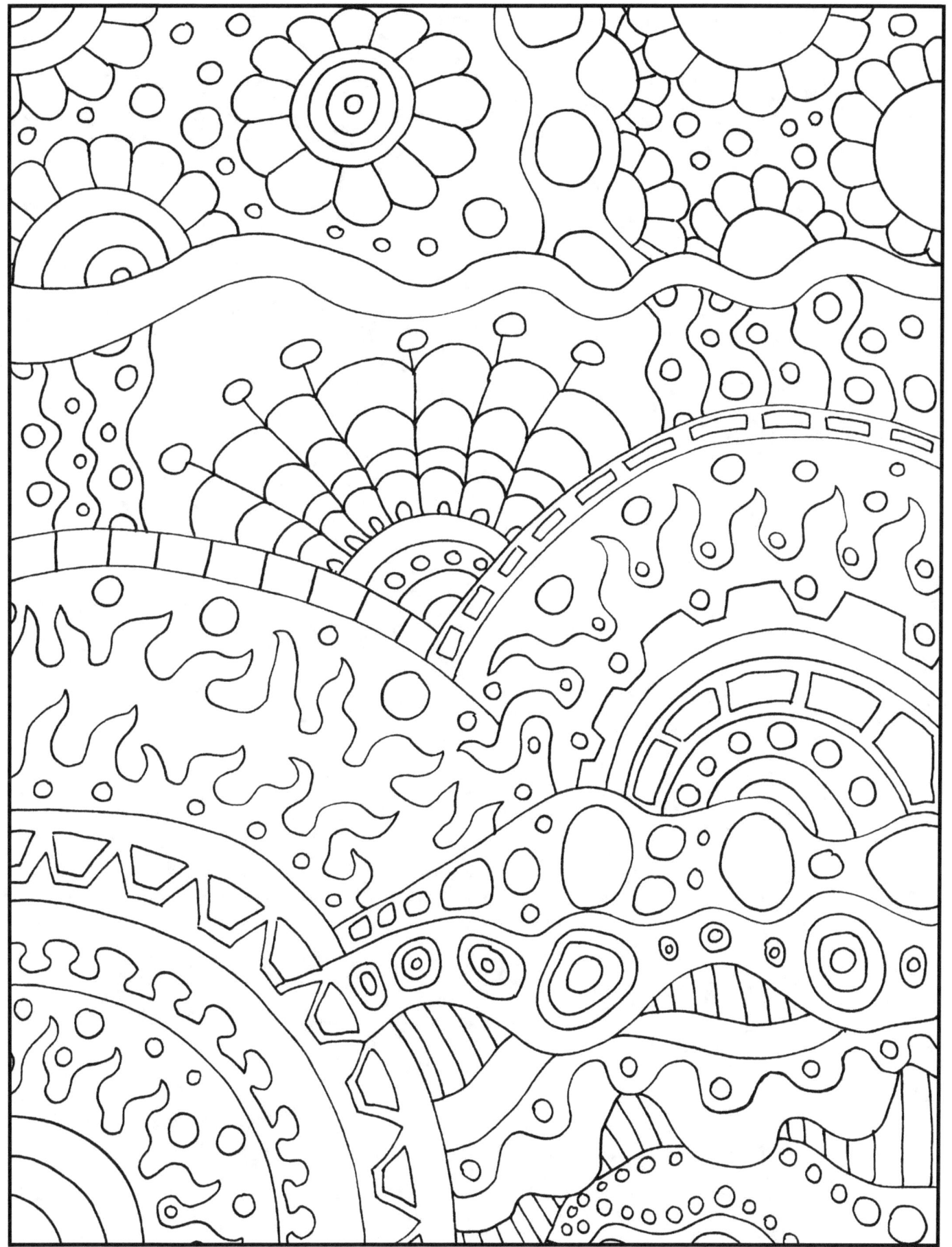

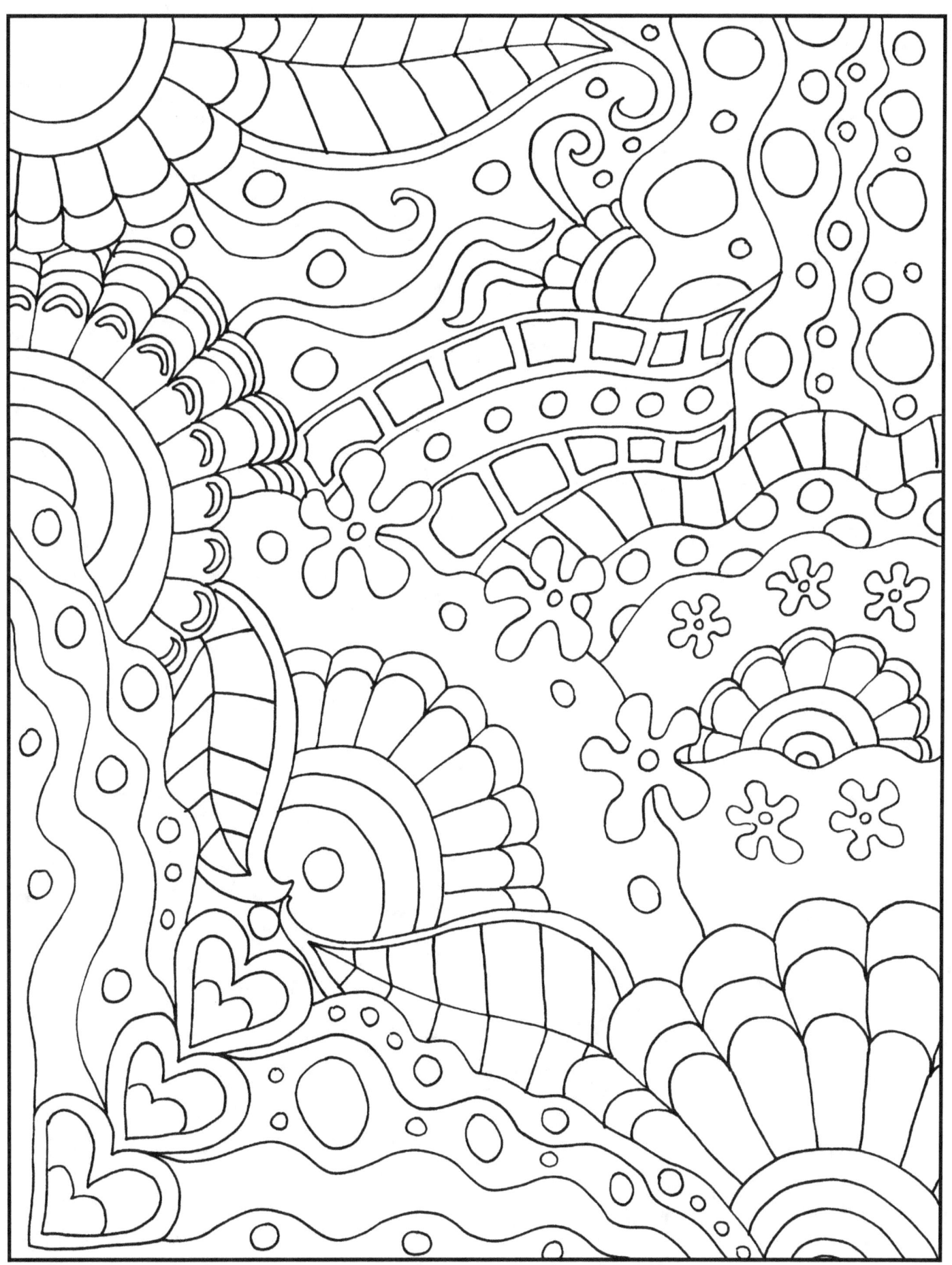

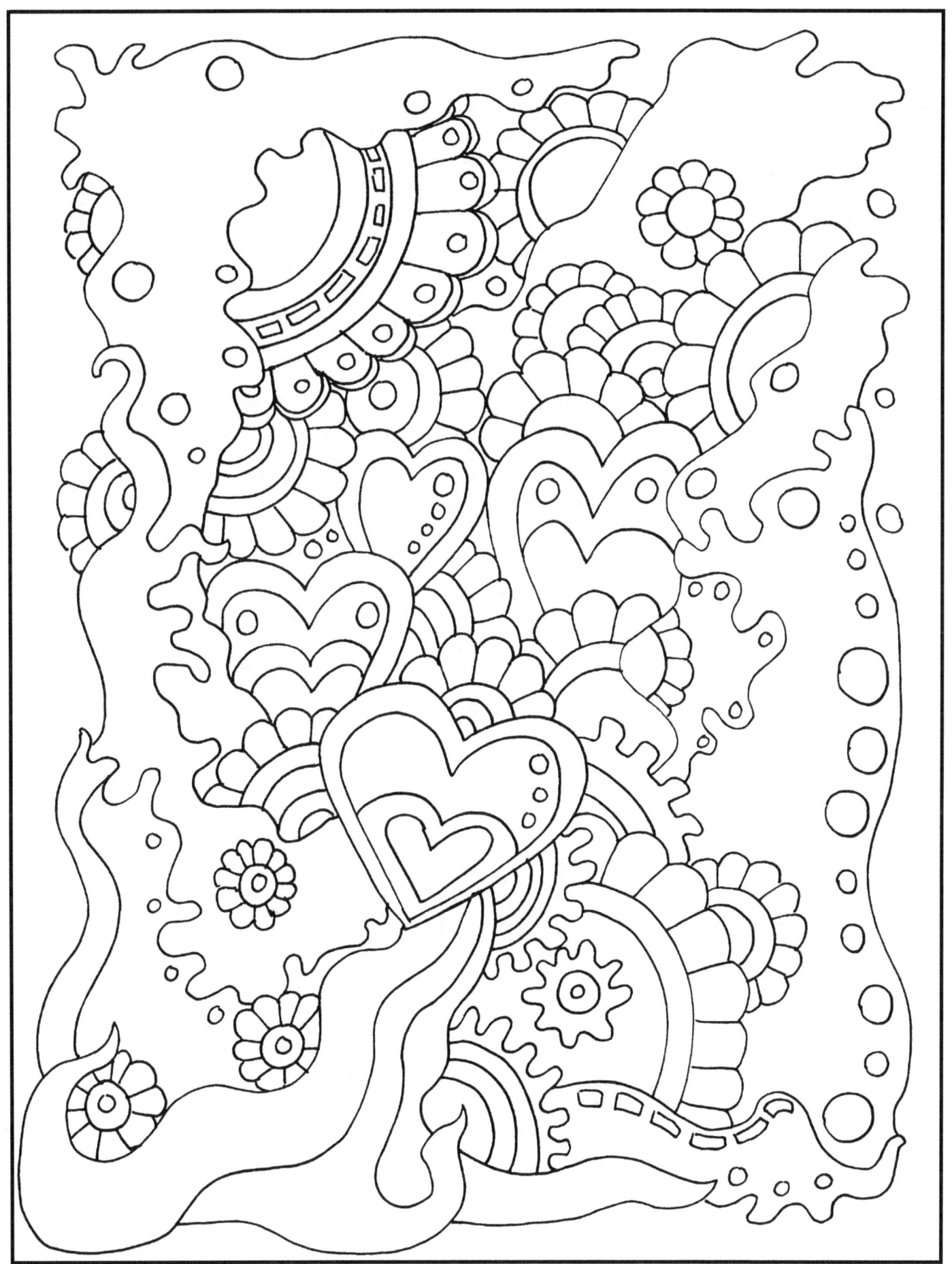

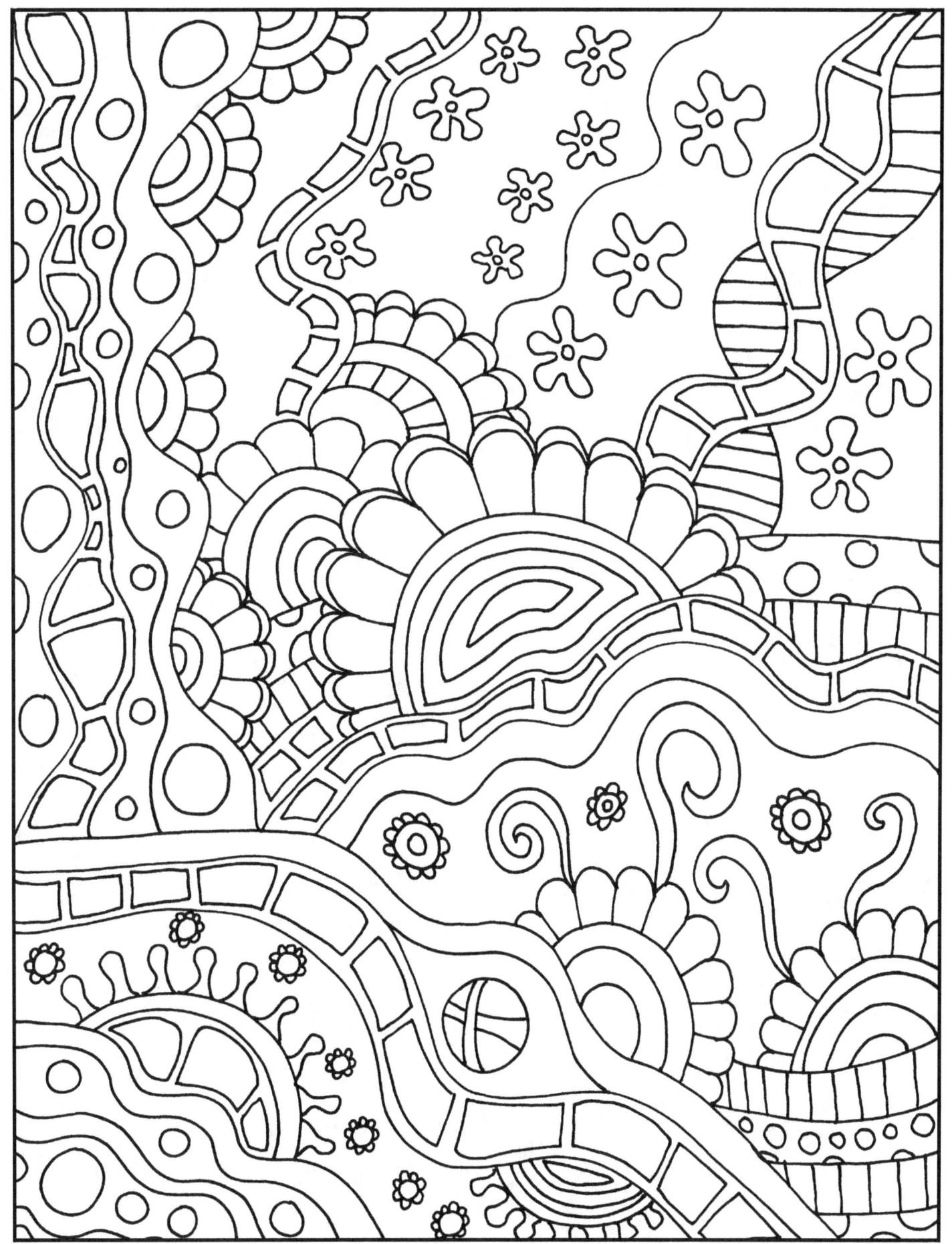

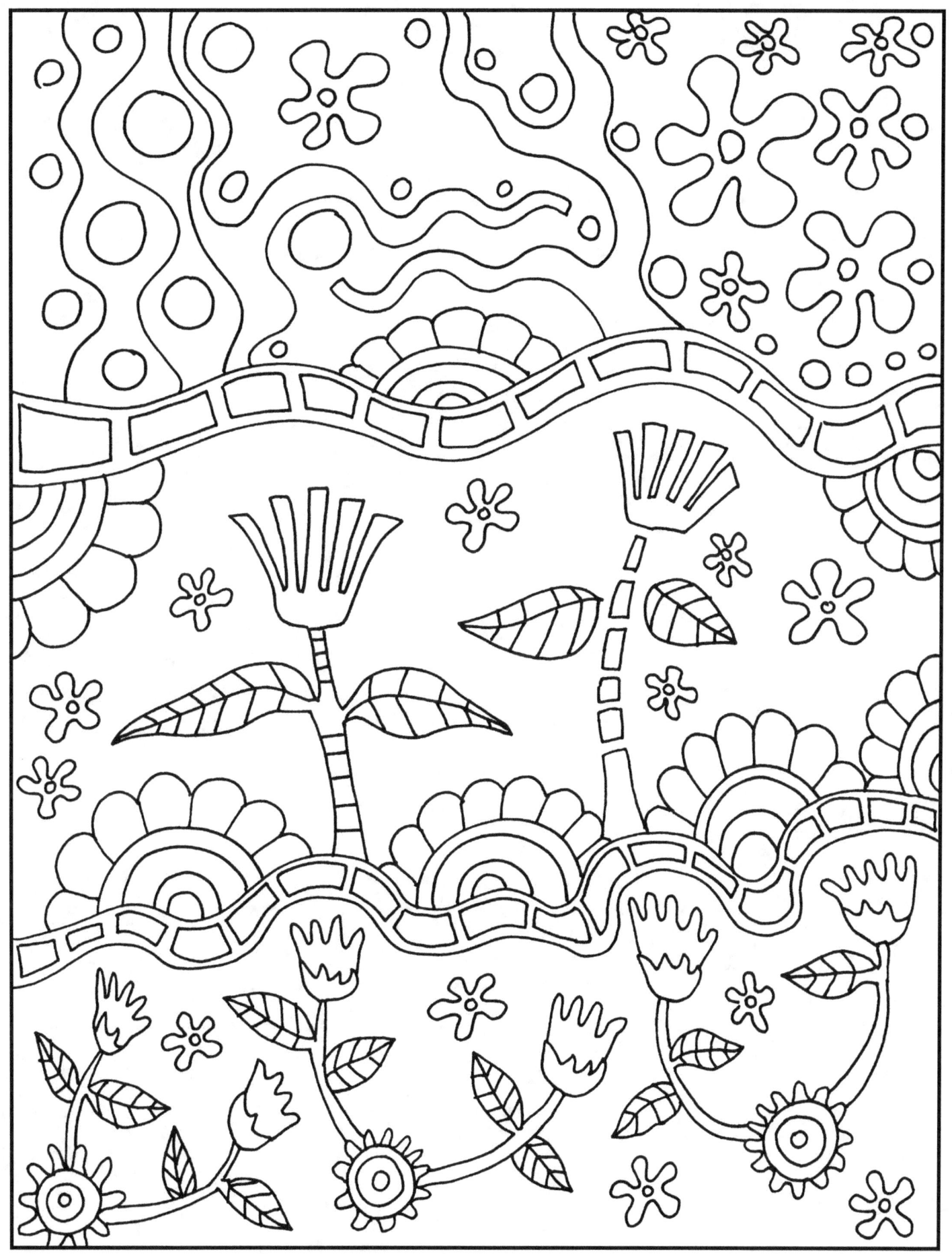

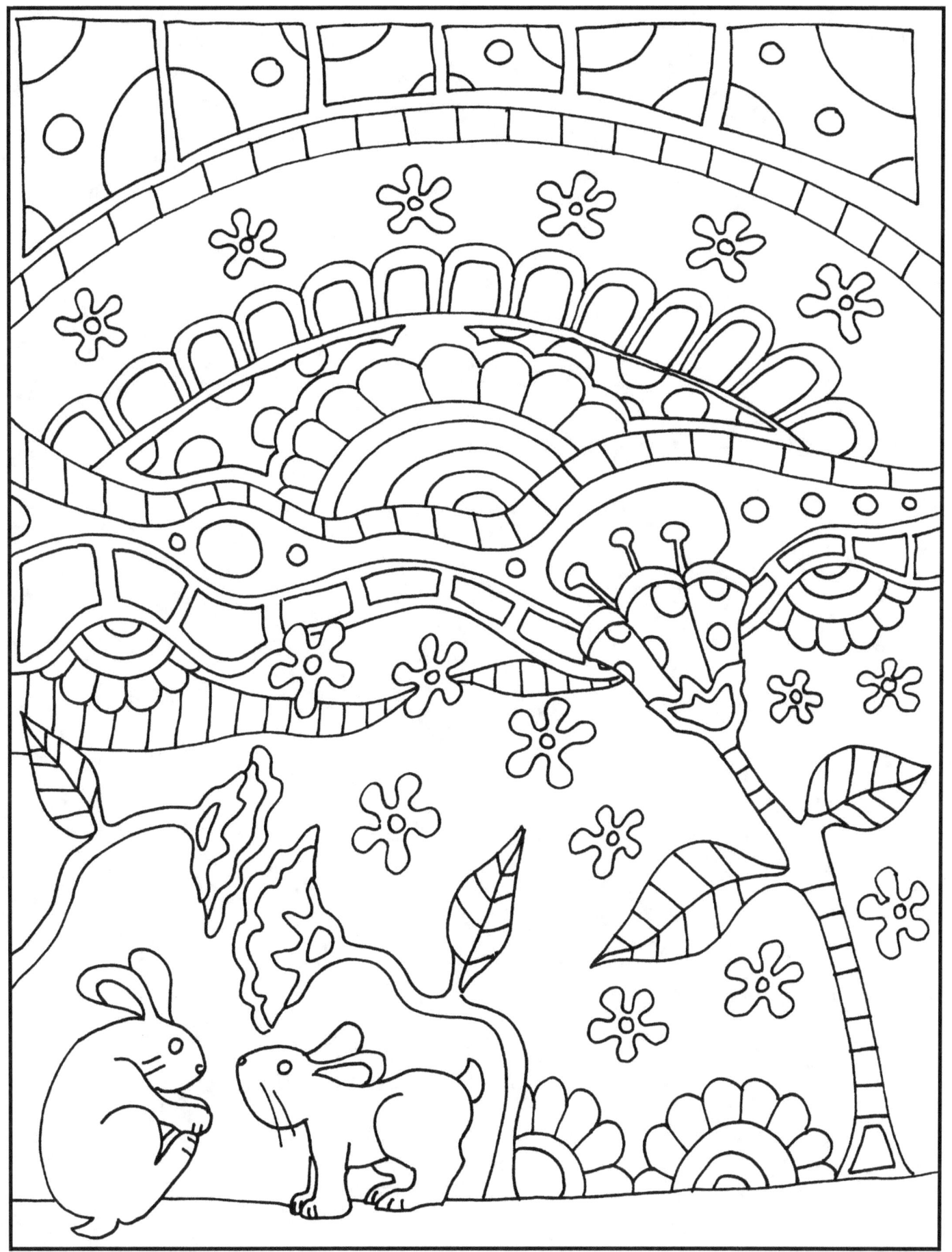

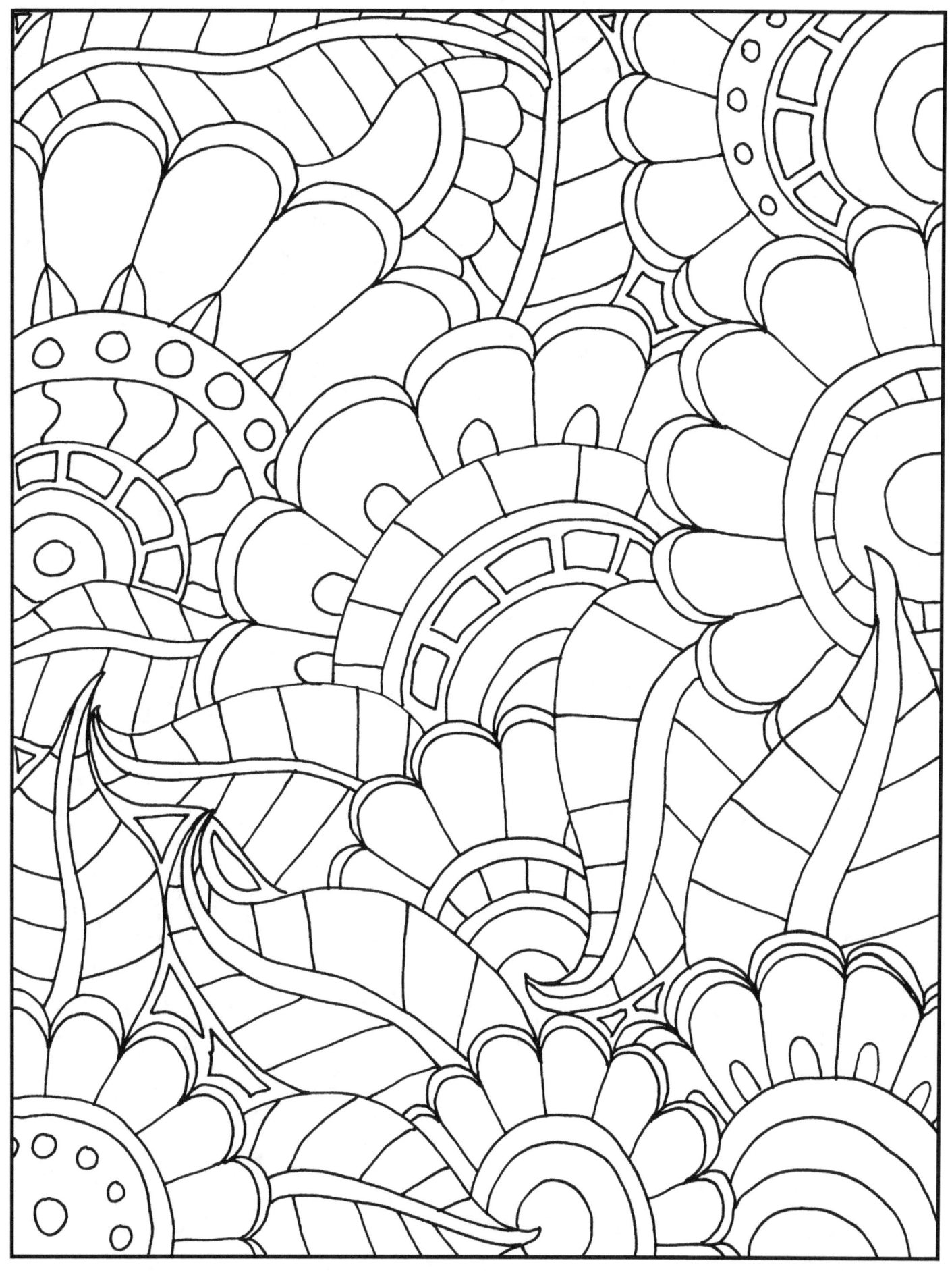

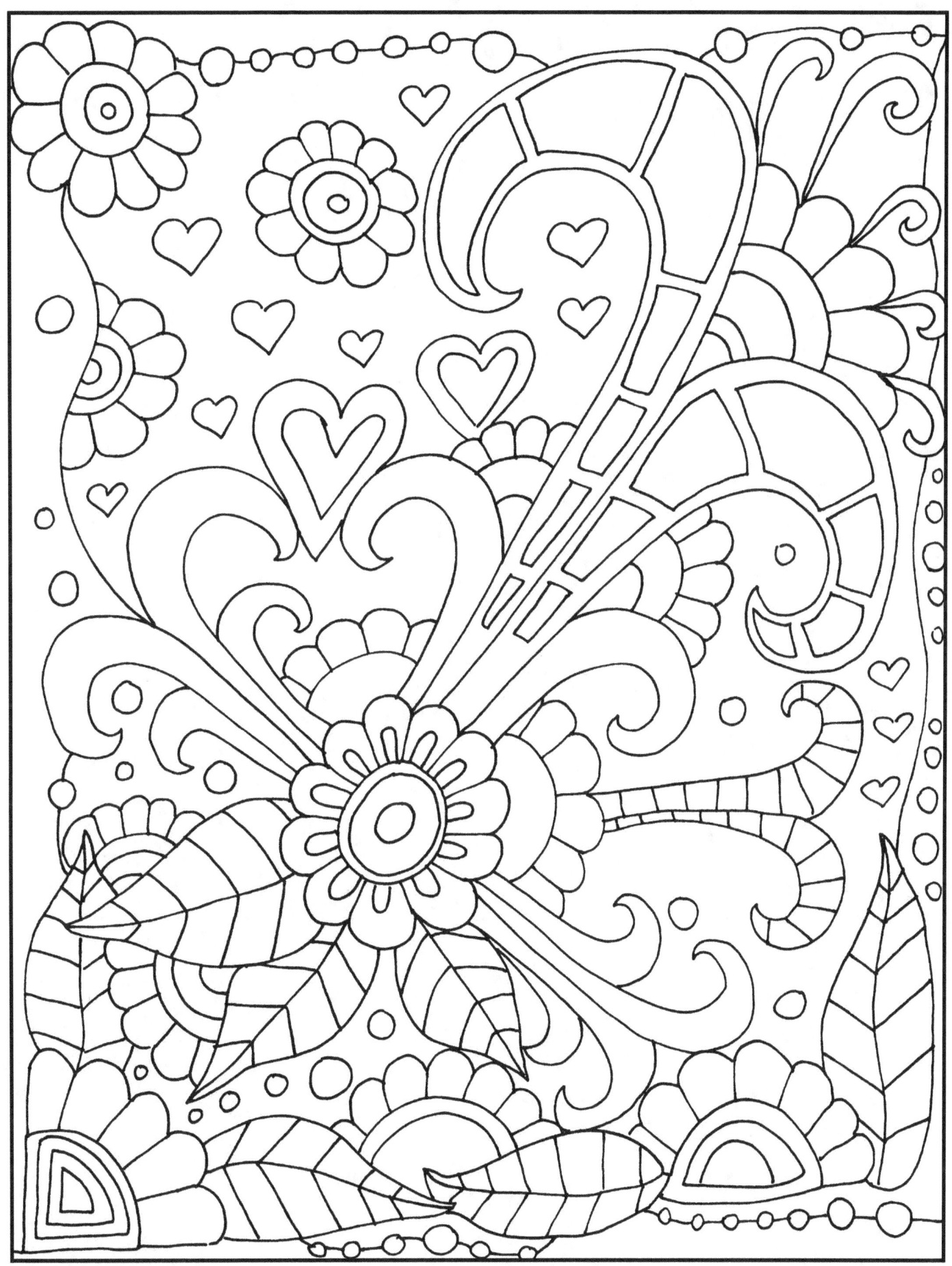

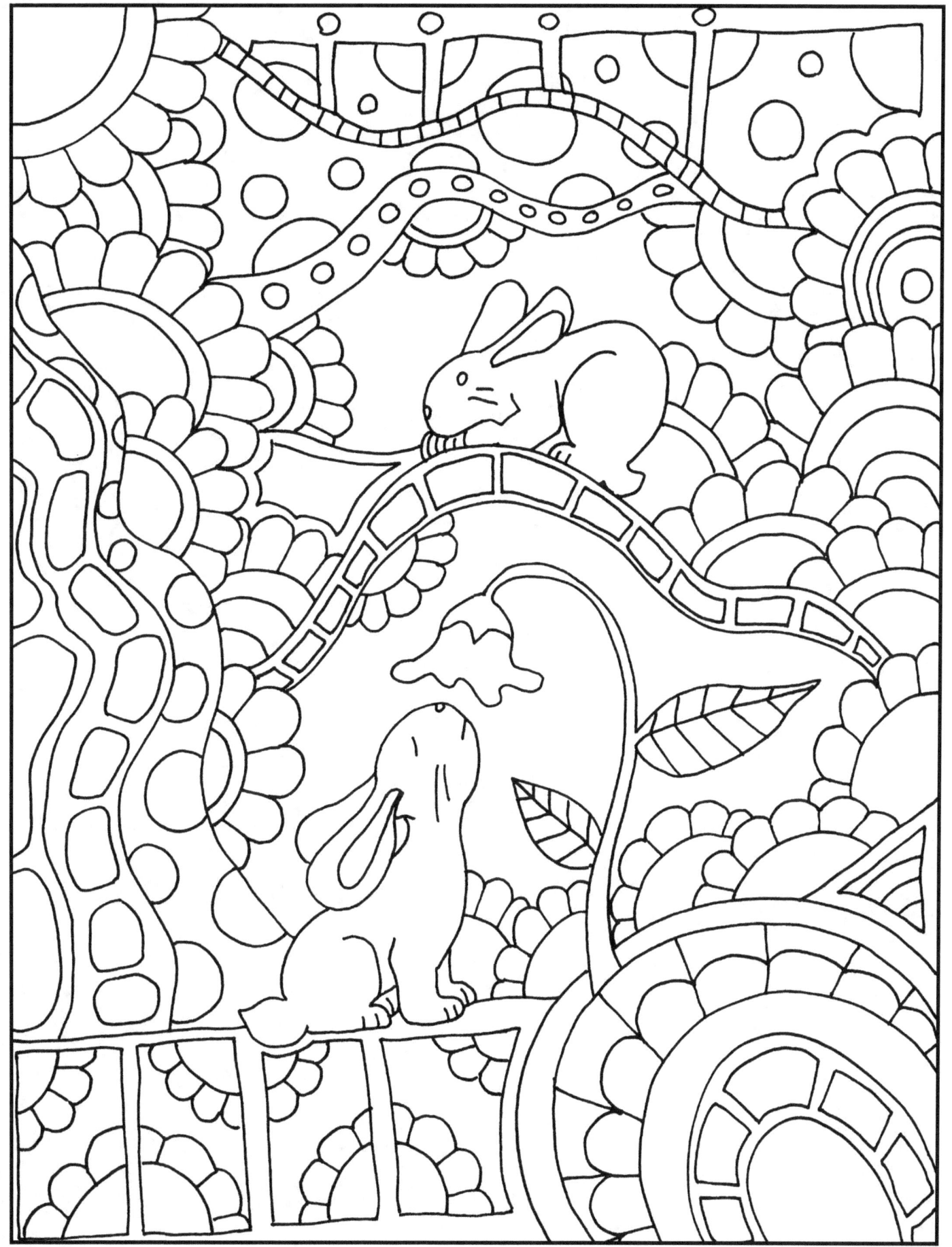

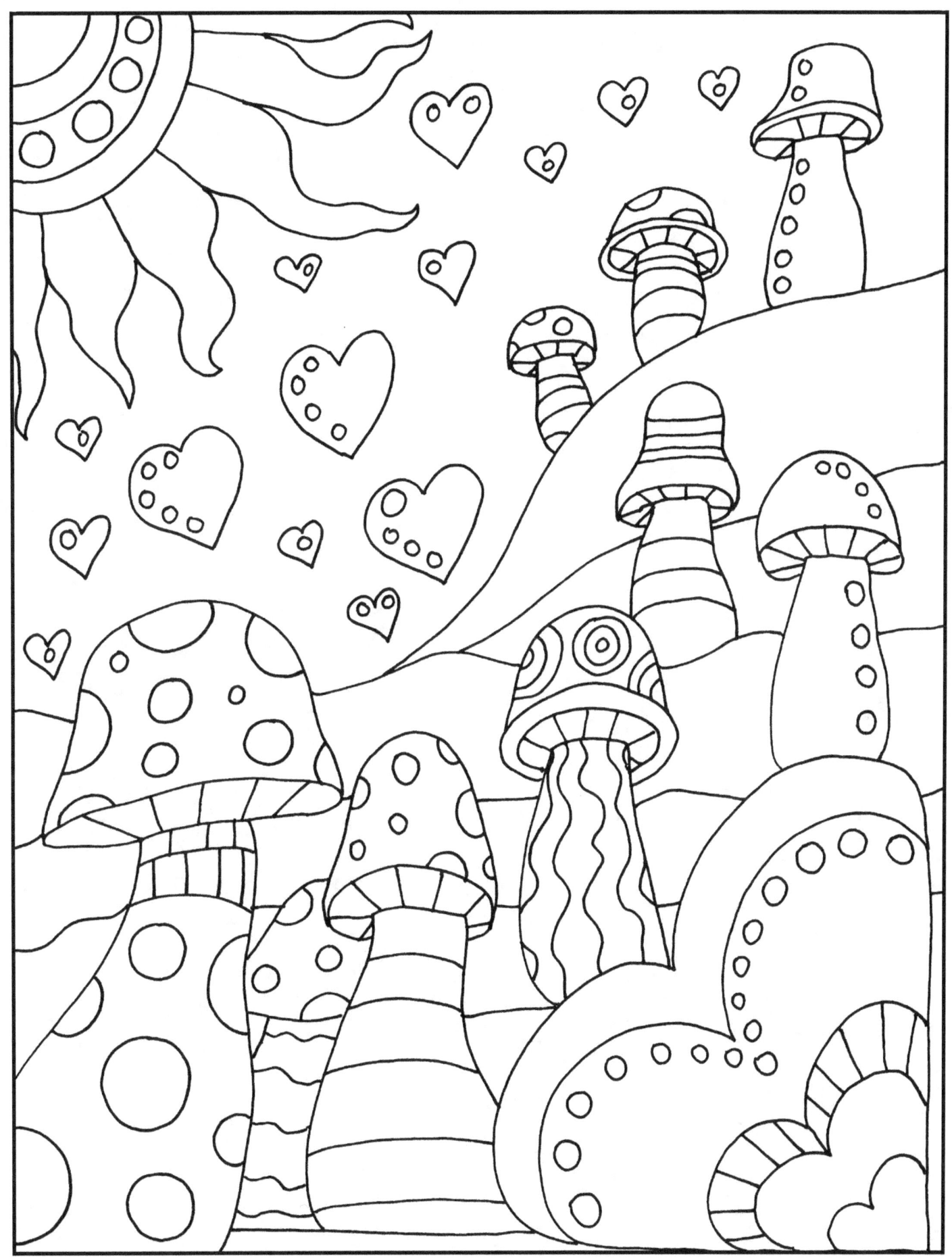

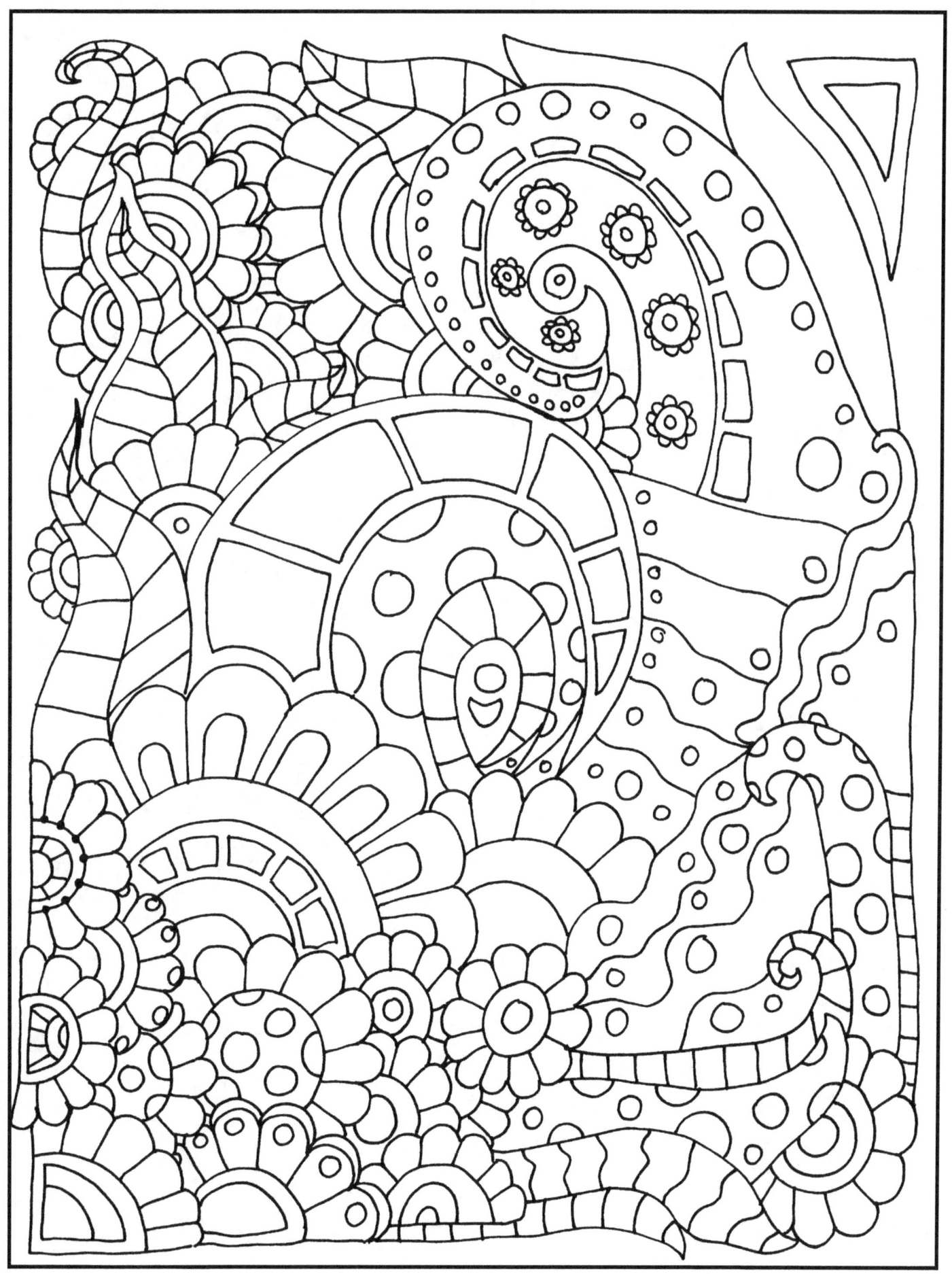

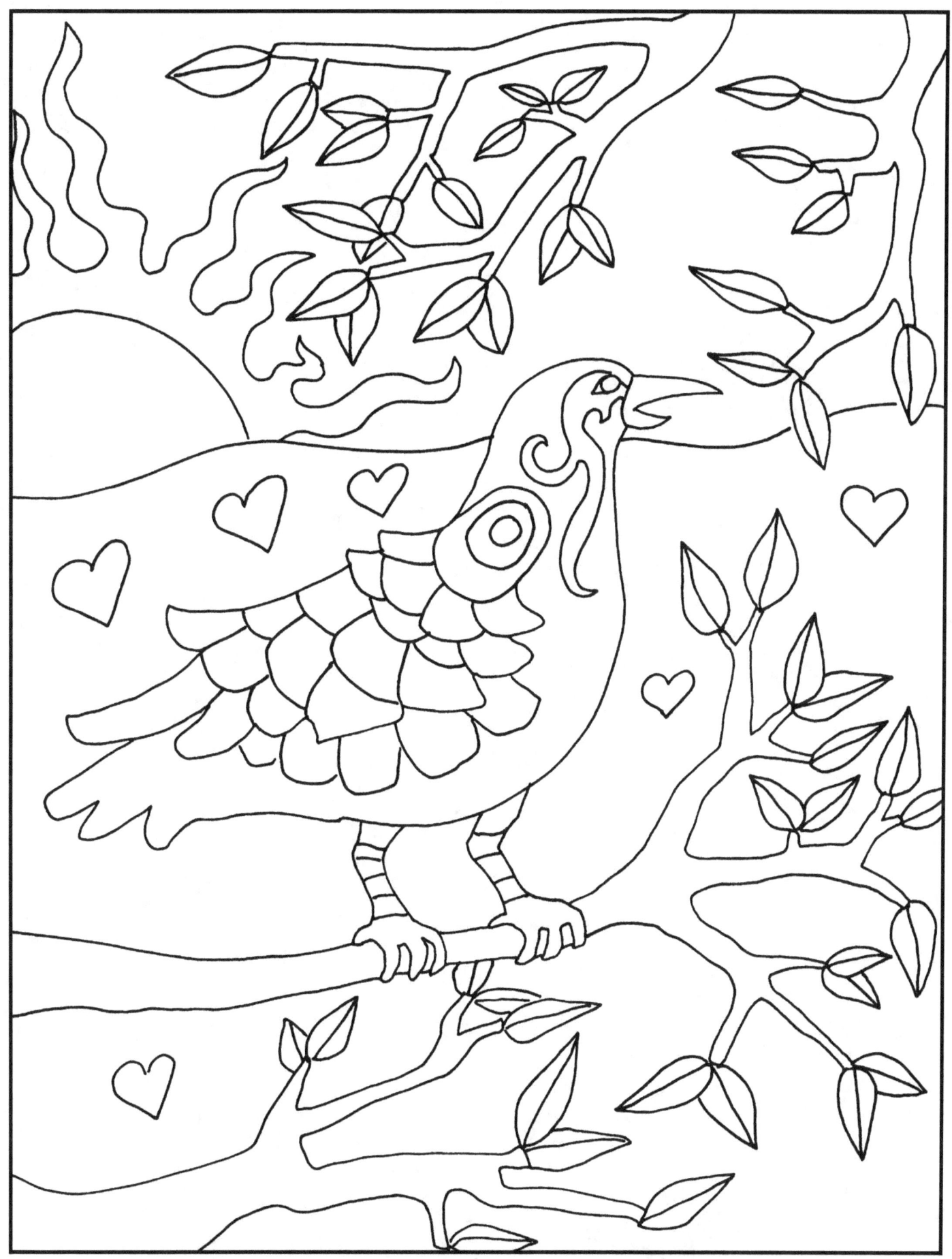

Also Available by Kimberly Garvey

- Strange Designs - An adult coloring book for everyone.

- Strange Little Designs - A mini/travel adult coloring book.

- **Simple Designs** - An adult coloring book with easier pages.

- **Simple Designs II** - Another adult coloring book with easier pages.

- Magical Daydreams - An adult coloring book for everyone.

- **It's Complicated** - A challenging. more detailed book for the daring colorists.

- The Fox Book - A foxy coloring book for everyone.

- **SUPER Simple Designs** - SUPER easy adult coloring

KIMBERLYGARVEY.COM

PROTECTION SHEET

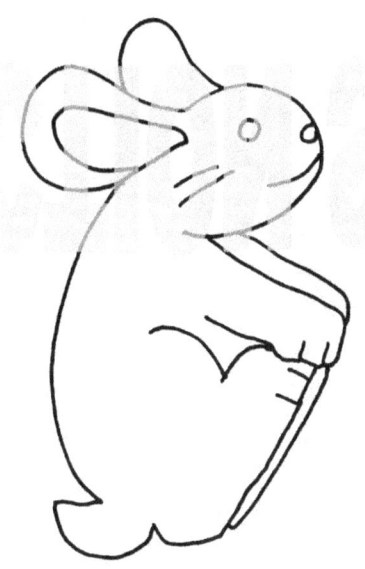

Place this page between coloring pages when using markers to prevent bleed-through.